NAACL HLT 2013 Workshop on Vision and Language

(WVL'13)

Atlanta, Georgia, USA
14 June 2013

ISBN: 978-1-62748-983-6

Printed from e-media with permission by:

Curran Associates, Inc.
57 Morehouse Lane
Red Hook, NY 12571

Some format issues inherent in the e-media version may also appear in this print version.

Printed by Curran Associates, Inc. (2013)

Association for Computational Linguistics
209 N. Eighth Street
Stroudsburg, Pennsylvania 18360

Phone: 1-570-476-8006
Fax: 1-570-476-0860

acl@aclweb.org

Additional copies of this publication are available from:

Curran Associates, Inc.
57 Morehouse Lane
Red Hook, NY 12571 USA
Phone: 845-758-0400
Fax: 845-758-2634
Email: curran@proceedings.com
Web: www.proceedings.com

Introduction

Welcome to the HLT NAACL Workshop on Vision and Language (WVL'13).

There is an increasing amount of research at the interfaces of speech and language processing and computer vision, computer graphics, robotics and information retrieval which aims to develop systems that automatically generate descriptions of images or videos, or generate images based on natural language descriptions, acquire and understand language in a perceptually grounded, visual context, or perform language-based image search.

Since the main purpose of this workshop is to bring researchers from these communities together, the workshop will mostly consist of invited talks, both by NLP and computer vision students who are working in the area, as well as by established researchers from academia and industry.

Organizers:

Julia Hockenmaier, University of Illinois at Urbana-Champaign
Tamara Berg, Stony Brook University

Program Committee:

Samy Bengio, Google
Alexander C Berg, Stony Brook University
Yejin Choi, Stony Brook University
Bill Dolan, Microsoft Research, Redmond
Jacob Eisenstein, Georgia Institute of Technology
Desmond Elliott, University of Edinburgh
Michel Galley, Microsoft Research, Redmond
Kristen Grauman, University of Texas, Austin
John Kelleher, Dublin Institute of Technology
Mirella Lapata, University of Edinburgh
Margaret Mitchell, Johns Hopkins University
Ray Mooney, University of Texas, Austin
Owen Rambow, Columbia University
Richard Sproat, Google

Table of Contents

Workshop Program

Friday, June 14, 2013

Session 1

8:45–9:00	Opening Remarks
9:00–10:00	Tutorial: *Computational Visual Recognition for NLP* Alexander C Berg (Stony Brook University)
10:00–10:30	Invited talk: *Modality Selection for Multimedia Summarization* Florian Metze (Carnegie Mellon University)
10:30–11:00	**Coffee break**

Session 2

11:00–11:20	*Annotation of Online Shopping Images without Labeled Training Examples* Rebecca Mason and Eugene Charniak
11:20–11:40	*Generating Natural-Language Video Descriptions Using Text-Mined Knowledge* Niveda Krishnamoorthy, Girish Malkarnenkar, Raymond Mooney, Kate Saenko and Sergio Guadarrama
11:40–12:00	*Learning Hierarchical Linguistic Descriptions of Visual Datasets* Roni Mittelman, Min Sun, Benjamin Kuipers and Silvio Savarese
12:00–12:30	Invited talk: *Joint Learning of Word Meanings and Image Tasks* Jason Weston (Google)
12:30–2:00	**Lunch Break**

Friday, June 14, 2013 (continued)

Session 3

2:00–2:15 Invited student talk:
Communicating with an Image Retrieval System via Relative Attributes
Adriana Kovashka and Kristen Grauman (University of Texas at Austin)

2:15–2:30 Invited student talk: *Identifying Visual Attributes for Object Recognition*
Caglar Tirkaz, Jacob Eisenstein, Berrin Yanikoglu and Metin Sezgin
(Sabanci University, Georgia Institute of Technology, Koc University)

2:30–2:45 Invited student talk: *Generating Visual Descriptions from Feature Norms of Actions, Attributes, Classes and Parts*
Mark Yatskar and Luke Zettlemoyer (University of Washington)

2:45–3:00 Invited student talk: *Bayesian modeling of scenes and captions*
Luca del Pero and Kobus Barnard (University of Arizona)

3:00–3:15 Invited student talk: *Data-Driven Generation of Image Descriptions*
Vicente Ordonez and Tamara Berg (Stony Brook University)

3:15–3:30 Invited student talk: *Framing image description as a retrieval problem*
Micah Hodosh, Peter Young and Julia Hockenmaier
(University of Illinois at Urbana-Champaign)

Session 4

4:00–4:30 Invited talk: *Multimodal Semantics at CLIC*
Elia Bruni (University of Trento)

4:30–5:00 Invited talk: *Generating and Generalizing Image Captions*
Yejin Choi (Stony Brook University)

5:00–5:30 Invited talk: *Generating Descriptions of Visible Objects*
Margaret Mitchell (Johns Hopkins University)

5:30–6:00 Panel discussion
Julia Hockenmaier and Tamara Berg

Annotation of Online Shopping Images without Labeled Training Examples

Rebecca Mason and **Eugene Charniak**
Brown Laboratory for Linguistic Information Processing (BLLIP)
Brown University, Providence, RI 02912
{rebecca,ec}@cs.brown.edu

Abstract

We are interested in the task of image annotation using noisy natural text as training data. An image and its caption convey different information, but are generated by the same underlying concepts. In this paper, we learn latent mixtures of topics that generate image and product descriptions on shopping websites by adapting a topic model for multilingual data (Mimno et al., 2009). We use the trained model to annotate test images without corresponding text. We capture visual properties such as color, texture, shape, and orientation by computing low-level image features, and measure the contribution of each type of visual feature towards the accuracy of the model. Our model significantly outperforms both a competitive baseline and a previous topic model-based system.

1 Introduction

Image annotation is a classic problem in Computer Vision. Given a query image, the task is to generate a set of textual labels that describe the visual content. The typical approach to these problems is to use supervised models, which require large numbers of hand-annotated examples for each of the labels. However, the amount of information available on the web continues to grow, the task of organizing and describing visual data becomes increasingly complex. For example, a shopping website might arrange products into broad categories such as "shoes" and "handbags" with each category containing tens of thousands of products that are difficult for users to search and navigate. It is often infeasible to discover all of the attributes within those categories that are relevant to users and create labeled training examples for each of them.

Instead, we approach this problem by discovering visual attributes from noisy natural language captions. That is, given a collection of images and captions found on the web, we learn a model of visual and textual features. Then given a query image with no text, we can generate likely descriptive words. This is a difficult task because image captions on the web are often noisy and incomplete: some captions might not describe a particular visual feature, might use a synonym for that feature, or might describe information that is not visual in the image at all.

A secondary motivation for this work is to use the image annotations as a component in language generation systems such as for automatic image captioning. We point to examples of previous work such as Feng and Lapata (2010a) where image annotations generated from a topic model are used to help generate full sentences to describe images. Much of the current research in image captioning is limited by the current technology for object recognition in Computer Vision. For example, SBU-Flickr dataset (Ordonez et al., 2011) with 1 million images and captions, is considered to be general-domain but is actually built by querying Flickr using a pre-defined term list related to visual attributes that there are trained recognition systems for. While these systems can accurately generate descriptions for common visual objects and attributes, they are not as well-suited for describing the "long-tail" of visual attributes which appear in many domain-specific

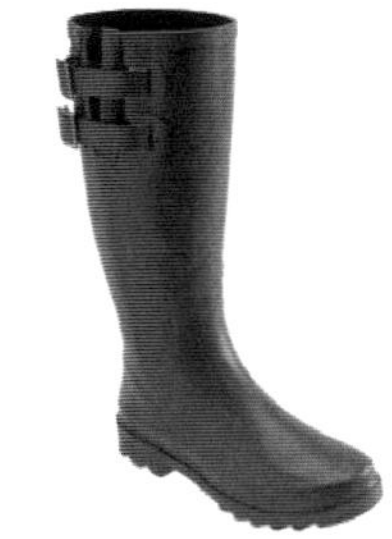		
Two adjustable buckle straps top a classic rubber rain boot grounded by a thick lug sole for excellent wet-weather traction.	Size(s) Available: 6, 11.5. Brand & Style - VANS Kvd Width - Medium (B, M) Heel Height - Shoe Size is Womens Size 11.5 = Mens Size 10 1 Inch Heel Material - Canvas Upper and Man Made Sole	Carlo Fellini - Evening clutch beaded on a wave pattern

Table 1: Examples of data from the Attribute Discovery Dataset (Berg et al., 2010). The images are fairly clean and uniform, while captions have more noise and variation.

datasets.

In this paper, we model image and text features from the training data using a generative model. We adapt the Polylingual topic model from Mimno et al. (2009) to train on multi-modal data, and then use the trained model to generate annotations for test images. We evaluate our model on two categories of shopping images using a variety of types of computed image features. For image annotation we outperform both a difficult baseline and previous work.

2 Related Work

We use the polylingual topic model from Mimno et al. (2009), which was developed to model multilingual corpora that are *topically comparable* between languages – the documents are not direct translations, but they cover the same ideas. For example, English and Finnish Wikipedia pages about skiing are roughly similar, but the subject is covered more thoroughly in Finnish. Therefore, the number of tokens assigned to the Finnish topic for skiing is much higher than it is in the English. While Mimno et al. (2009) show that the model is effective in tasks such as modeling topically comparable documents across languages, our work is the first to show that this model can be used to model data of different *modalities*. Another quality of the polylingual topic model is that words in different languages do not directly correspond with each other. This is a feature of other multi-lingual topic models but would not work for multi-modal data because a textual word can carry more meaning by itself than an image feature can.

Countless approaches have been proposed for the use of topic models in image annotation, but the vast majority of these approaches consider the text modality merely as labels for the image modality. The most highly cited of these is the Correspondence LDA (corr-LDA) model of Blei et al. (2003), where topics are learned using the image modality alone, and each textual word must be generated by a specific region in the image. However, more recent work has started to recognize the textual modality as a source of information in its own right. Jia et al. (2011) present a model that allows different information to be emphasized in each modality, but it requires very clean text; they do not use documents with captions that cannot be easily parsed or processed. Then, they stem all words, and disregard sparse word tokens. This works when working with sources such as Wikipedia, where text captions are highly edited and consistently formatted. In comparision, our work can be trained on corpra where the text has poor or inconsistant quality. Additionally, their work was for the task of image retrieval from a text query, while we are generating text annotations for a query image.

Our work is most similar to the MixLDA model of Feng and Lapata (2010b), except MixLDA models images and their related text as a single bag-of-features, with visual and textual features coming from the same vocabulary. This means that some topics should have a greater proportion of features from one of modalities, if there is an idea that is better expressed in one over the other. Their model was developed for finding descriptive words given both an image and a news article, and can also be used on large and noisy amounts of data, so we compare MixLDA against our model in the experiments.

Although we use the Attribute Discovery Dataset of Berg et al. (2010), their work is different from ours in both problem formulation and the types of attributes discovered. Their primary interest is to characterize attributes according to how they are visually represented: global or local; color, texture, or shape. Their work does not address the task of predicting attributes for unseen images. Additionally, they do not work with individual descriptive words, but cluster them using mutual information of visual attributes, creating a smaller number of "visual synsets". For example, one of their visual synsets for images and descriptions of womens handbags is {*mesh, interior, metal*} and another is {*silver, metallic*}. In comparison, in the topic model the same word can be generated by more than one topic.

Liu et al. (2010) examine the use of a variety of image features in a Bayesian model in order to measure which are the best for classifying diverse materials such as stone, glass, and plastic. They found that the image features they used for shape and color were better indicators of the material of an object than texture features, and their best combined model did not include texture as a feature at all. We are also interested in finding out whether our performance on generating descriptive words is affected by different types of image features.

3 Dataset

We use the Attribute Discovery Dataset from Berg et al. (2010).[1] The dataset consists of pairs of images and captions taken from the shopping website `like.com`. The data has four categories: women's shoes, handbags, earrings, and neckties. We run our model on two categories, shoes and handbags, due to their larger sizes – 14764 and 9145 image-caption pairs respectively – and diversity of features. This is a reasonable amount of data in the shopping images domain; more than half of the number of comparable products sold on large retail websites such as `Zappos.com` or `Amazon.com`.

Compared to general datasets such as Pascal Sentences, the images in the Attribute Discovery Dataset are more uniform. All image files are 280x280 pixel JPEGs, and images of products are typically taken from similar angles against a white or a light-colored solid background. Only rarely do the images have noisy backgrounds, such as a person wearing the item, or the same item displayed in multiple colors in one image. However, this does not necessarily make our task much easier, since the visual attributes we wish to learn are not pre-defined as they are in a general-domain dataset. And the lack of hand-annotated data means no *negative examples* of when an attribute is not present, which are typically used to train visual classifiers.

Furthermore, the captions are extremely noisy in this dataset. Compared to the 20 object types in the Pascal Sentences dataset, or about one hundred in COREL, here there are thousands of words that can be used to describe features in the images, including synonyms, multiple stems of words, and misspellings. In addition to explicit visual descriptions of the products, the captions describe "less visual" features such as details about the construction of the item, during which season or activity it would be appropriate to wear, or feelings that could be evoked by looking at the item. These features are difficult to represent as specific visual attributes, but can be identified visually by domain-experts. Captions can also include information that is non-visual such as sizing and shipping information, or whether the item is on sale.

The captions can be either full English sentences, a list of features, or sometimes just a few words. Longer captions in the dataset are truncated to 250 characters in length.

From our own obervations, we estimate about 10% of the captions in the shoes dataset contain few or no descriptive words. At least 3.7% of the shoes captions are entirely Javascript code, have significant portions of code, or very long URLs. Another 5-6% either contain no information besides

[1] `http://tamaraberg.com/attributesDataset/index.html`

sizing or shipping information, only the brand name or model number of the shoe, or the caption is so short that there are only one or two descriptive words that could be used in our model. In the womens' shoes category, we take some simple steps to remove URLs and code to avoid learning accidental correlation with legitimate features.[2] However, we still use all image and caption pairs in the training set, including those which end up having empty captions, since they are still useful for learning topics for visual features. For the handbags captions, we did not try to remove code or long URLs since it seemed to be less of a problem in that category.

4 Feature Representation

4.1 Text Features

The bag-of-words model is used for text. We use Mxterminator (Reynar and Ratnaparkhi, 1997) to split sentences in the captions (in many instances, nothing is done in this step becuase there are no full sentences in the caption), Stanford POS Tagger(Toutanova et al., 2003) to tag words, then include adjectives, adverbs, verbs, and nouns in the topic model (except for proper nouns and common background English words from a stoplist). However, these tags are really more a rough estimate of parts of speech due to the number of incomplete sentences and phrases, and the fact that many of the words used to describe styles or attributes of clothing have different meanings in colloqueal English.[3]

All tokens are converted to lower case, but there is no stemming or lemmatization. After preprocessing, the size of the shoes text vocabulary is 9578 words, with an average of 16.33 descriptive words per image, while the bags have a text vocabulary of 6309 word types with 15.41 descriptive words per image on average.

4.2 Visual Features

The bag-of-features model is used for visual features as well. Most of these features are standard in computer vision research, and are also used in work we cited in Section 2.

[2]Tokens removed: URLs, all tokens that end in ".sh", and a few tokens obviously related to Javascript eg *script, src, typeof, var*.

[3]Some examples of domain-specific words used in shopping image descriptions: `www.zappos.com/glossary`

Shape: A SIFT descriptor describes which way edges are oriented at a certain point in an image (Lowe, 1999). It was develped to recognize the same object under different scales and rotations. However, it is also commonly used for recognizing more generalized types or features of objects. We use the VLFeat open source library (Vedaldi and Fulkerson, 2008) to compute SIFT features at points of interest and to cluster the SIFT features into discrete "visual terms" using the k-means algorithm. There are 750 visual terms for SIFT features.

Color: We use two representations for color, RGB (red, green, blue) and HSV (hue, saturation, value). 25 pixels are sampled from the center 100x100 pixels of the image (to avoid sampling from the background of the image). Those pixel values are also clustered to visual terms using k-means, with 100 visual terms each.

Texture: Images are convolved with Gabor filters at multiple orientations and scales, sampled at random locations, then clustered to form *texton* features for texture (Leung and Malik, 2001). We convert all images to grayscale, then sample 25 locations from the center of the image, and cluster to 100 visual terms. We also have a color texton feature, where we sample and cluster textons separately for the red, green, and blue color channels.

Reflectance/Curvature:[4] We use three types of related features for gradients and curvature. The first is a bag-of-HOG (histogram of gradients) feature set (Dalal and Triggs, 2005) computed over a regular grid on the image to measure changes in intensity.[5] The most significant of those features (as determined by L^2 norm) are selected for each image, and like previous features are clustered into visual terms using k-means. The second two types are derivatives of HOG which include information about the amount of curvature at each orientation of the HOG descriptor.[6]

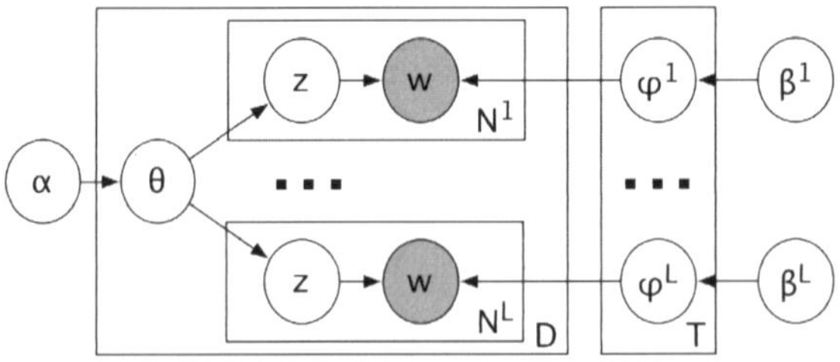

Figure 1: Polylingual topic model (Mimno et al., 2009)

5 Model

We model textual and visual features using the polylingual topic model by Mimno et al. (2009). In this section, we describe how the generative process and inference of this model is adapted to topically comparable multi-modal data.

Figure 1 shows the original polylingual topic model. We model multi-modal data using two "languages": *txt* for the bag-of-words captions, and *img* for the combined visual terms. The generative process is defined for an image and caption pair, $w =< w^{img}, w^{txt} >$:

$$\theta \sim Dir(\theta, \alpha m)$$

$$z^{img} \sim P(z^{img}|\theta) = \prod_n \theta_{z_n^{img}}$$

$$z^{txt} \sim P(z^{txt}|\theta) = \prod_n \theta_{z_n^{txt}}$$

$$w^{img} \sim P(w^{img}|z^{img}, \Phi^{img}) = \phi^{img}_{w_n^{img}|z_n^{img}}$$

$$w^{txt} \sim P(w^{txt}|z^{txt}, \Phi^{txt}) = \phi^{txt}_{w_n^{txt}|z_n^{txt}}$$

First, a topic distribution for w is drawn from an asymmetric Dirichlet prior with concentration parameter α and base measure m. Then a latent topic assignment is drawn for each word token in w^{txt}, and each discrete image feature in w^{img}. Once the topic assignments are sampled, the observed tokens are sampled according to their probability in the modality-specific topics $\Phi^{img} = \{\phi_1^{img}, ..., \phi_T^{img}\}$ and $\Phi^{txt} = \{\phi_1^{txt}, ..., \phi_T^{txt}\}$.

[4]Note: These features are implemented using code from (Felzenszwalb et al.,).

[5]There is significant overlap between these features, although the benefits of overlap are lost due to the bag-of-features model.

[6]Personal correspondance, work in progress.

To find the most probable descriptive words for an unseen image, the first step is to estimate the topic distribution that generated the image. Gibbs sampling is used to sample topic assignments for visual terms in the test image d^{img}:

$$P(z_n = t|d^{img}, z_{\setminus n}, \Phi^{img}, \alpha m)$$

$$\propto \phi^{img}_{d_n^{img}|t} \frac{(N_t)_{\setminus n} + \alpha m_t}{\sum_t N_t - 1 + \alpha}$$

Assuming that the descriptive words are independent, the probability of text word w_i given d^{img} is:

$$P(w_i|d^{img}) = \sum_t P(w_i|z_t^{txt})P(z_t|d^{img})$$

summing over all topics $t \in T$.

For training the model, we used the Polylingual topic model implementation from the Mallet toolkit (McCallum, 2002) (with some small modifcations to use it for generation). We use 1000 iterations for inference, with hyperparameter optimization every 10 iterations. In both shoes and bags categories, the number of topics is 200, which was minimally tuned by hand on the shoes data.

6 Experimental Setup and Evaluation

We first run our model on the larger category, shoes. For both systems and baselines, we find the 10, 15, and 20 most likely words for the test images. We evaluate by computing precision and recall against descriptive words from the held-out captions for those images.[7] We compute macro-averages of these scores because there is a lot of variation between the sizes of the captions in the dataset. The split between training and test instances is 80/20%.

We also evaluate the contributions of different types of image features. We evaluate the model for each image feature individually (along with the text features), as well as combinations of image features.

We compare against the MixLDA system and a strong baseline. We choose MixLDA because it is relatively easy to re-implement and because it

[7]We find descriptive words for test instances in the exact same way we did for training instances in Section 4.1. Instances where we did not find any useable descriptive words did not count towards the evaluation.

	10 words			15 words			20 words		
	P	**R**	**F1**	**P**	**R**	**F1**	**P**	**R**	**F1**
Baselines									
MixLDA	21.02	13.80	16.66	17.41	17.15	17.13	14.88	19.53	16.89
Corpus frequency	21.03	13.73	16.61	17.51	17.14	17.32	15.41	20.12	17.45
Single Attribute									
SIFT	27.00	16.30	20.34	22.84	20.65	21.69	20.09	24.22	21.96
Grayscale Texture	21.26	13.88	16.80	18.25	17.87	18.06	15.71	20.52	17.80
RGB Texture	24.77	14.93	18.63	21.01	18.99	19.95	18.49	22.29	20.21
HSV Color	22.17	13.35	16.67	18.59	16.79	17.65	16.48	19.85	18.01
RGB Color	23.21	13.98	17.45	19.78	17.88	18.78	17.53	21.12	19.15
HOG	26.33	15.87	19.80	22.36	20.21	21.23	19.60	23.62	21.42
TriHOG	24.60	14.82	18.50	20.64	18.66	19.60	18.14	21.87	19.83
TriHOG-Polar	26.03	15.69	19.58	22.06	19.94	20.95	19.32	23.29	21.12
Combined Models									
All-Color	24.22	14.60	18.22	20.62	18.65	19.59	18.11	21.83	19.80
All-Texture	25.50	15.41	19.24	21.63	19.55	20.53	18.88	22.75	20.64
All-HOG	27.36	16.50	20.58	23.31	21.07	22.14	20.40	24.58	22.30
Combine All	29.31	17.70	22.04	24.88	22.49	23.63	21.71	26.16	23.73
SIFT+RGB Texture+HOG	28.62	17.25	21.52	24.35	22.01	23.12	21.20	25.55	23.17

Table 2: Results of evaluation in the women's shoes cateogory (top 10-20 words).

has previously outperformed other image annotation systems when trained on natural language captions. Because the MixLDA model originally only used SIFT features, we compare it against the SIFT-only version of our model, with each system using the same computed image and text features. We re-implement the MixLDA system mostly as it is described in Feng and Lapata (2010b), with a few changes to make it more comparable to our model: Obviously in our version of MixLDA the test instances are only the unseen image as there is no other surrounding text. The number of topics is 200 (the original MixLDA had more but that did not seem to help here), and the α and β hyperparameters are optimized every 10 iterations.[8]

We also compare our model against corpus frequency of words in the training set. Although this may seem like a trivial baseline, previous work on image annotation from both computer vision (Müller et al., 2002; Monay and Gatica-Perez, 2003; Barnard et al., 2003) and natural language processing (Mason and Charniak, 2012) has shown that a large portion of the keyword probability mass can often be accounted for by a very small number of words, allowing systems to game better-looking results by simply guessing the frequency distribution of the text vocabulary. We find this to be especially true in the domain-specific case, where common terms (eg *shoe, sole, heel, upper*) are used in almost every caption, and in some captions account for most words used (such as the second example in Table 1). While domain-frequent words are also needed for generating new captions, we don't want them to account for all of the words our system generates. Of course, a human evaluation would be another possible way of addressing this issue, but it would be difficult and expensive to find enough people who have sufficient knowledge of womens' clothing and would be able to accurately say whether the generated words are appropriate or not (words such as *hobo, PU, stacked, upper,* and *vamp*). Also, although the gold image captions are noisy, the num-

[8]We used the Mallet toolkit's Parallel LDA sampler for inference, while a variational approach is used in the original. However, we do not believe this would change the outcome of this experiment. We also tried MixLDA without hyperparameter optimization but we do not show those results as they are significantly worse.

sole upper detail heel print fun fabric patent uppers soles high shoe rounded leather rubber lining elastic animal toe feet	style upper heel leather strap sandal lining toe dress satin shoe comfort ankle sole adjustable outsole platform stiletto rhinestone sandals	bag, leather, zip, pocket, hardware, features, shoulder, flap, main, cell, perfect, length, drop, zipper, closure, bold, phone, evening, holds, hobo
This high heel platform shoe has a patent leather upper with an ornamenting bow at the toe, a leather lining, a rounded toe, and a rubber bottom.Available Colors: Black Patent, Cheetah Print PU.	Create a timeless look with these Andie dress sandals from Coloriffics. Dyeable white satin matte satin or metallic satin upper in a two-piece dress-sandal style with an open round toe crossing pleated vamp straps with a dazzling rhinestone clasp and a wraparound heel strap with an adjustable buckle closure.	Treesje Dakota Shoulder Bag Black Shine - Designer Handbags

Table 3: Example results for unseen images. Both the top words generated by our model and the original held-out captions for the images are shown. (Note: In the third example, "hobo" is actually the term that is used to describe that shape of handbag.)

ber of test documents is very large so we can find significance on precision and recall using bootstrap resampling.

We also ran the baseline system and our system on the handbags category of the dataset. We did not modify the system in any way when using the bags dataset, just gave it different file for input.

7 Results and Discussion

The results of our evaluations are in Table 2. As we expected, the corpus frequency baseline does very well. It is comparable to MixLDA for 10 and 15 words, and significantly better than MixLDA for over 20 words. However, the Polylingual topic model using only SIFT features and text is much better than both. The trained MixLDA model has topics with both image and text features, so when estimating topics given only an image, it estimates that it was generated by topics that have a high proportion of image features. Though it also estimates some topics that have a mix of visual and text features, being able to generate good text descriptions from those topics, the topics that have less text features will be mainly determined by the smoothing parameter – the uniform distribution, worse than guessing the corpus distribution.

Out of the single attribute models, all except three of the single feaure models were significantly higher than corpus frequency on both precision and recall at 10, 15, and 20 words. The exceptions are the two color features and grayscale texture. For grayscale texture, we had expected it would correlate well with the material of the shoe; but either the low resolution of the images makes it difficult to distinguish materials by their texture, or materials don't correlate with the "less visual" features as much as we expected. Interestingly, since the material of an item tends to correlate strongly with other attributes such as shape and color, so our model still generates correct descriptive words for material in many cases.

While neither color nor texture were useful fea-

	10 words			15 words			20 words		
	P	**R**	**F1**	**P**	**R**	**F1**	**P**	**R**	**F1**
Corpus frequency	17.58	13.19	11.76	13.19	12.70	12.94	11.76	15.10	13.22
Combined Model	24.41	15.67	19.09	21.01	20.22	20.61	18.76	24.09	21.10

Table 4: Results of evaluation in the handbags cateogory (top 10-20 words).

tures on their own, RGB Texture did very well as a single attribute, and was within signficance of both the combined color and combined texture models. This may be related to the fact that RGB Textons have a larger number of visual terms than those other features, 100 for each of the three color channels. Unlike material, we observed that the color of an object is often not mentioned in the human-written caption (as seen in the examples in Table 1), or several colors are described in the caption where only one is seen in the image (seen in some of the examples in Table 3). We also observed that our system generates very few color words.

The gradient and shape-based features have the best single-attribute performance by far. Both SIFT and HOG capture shape at local points, but while SIFT features are invariant to differences in position or scale, HOG features are more sensitive to the way the item is oriented in the image. Although the curvature features TriHOG and TriHog-Polar are nearly as good as HOG on their own, combining the three HOG features does not significantly improve performance of the model over HOG alone.

Not all of the single-attribute models performed as well as others, but there was no case where removing one of the features improved the performance of the combined model. The fewest number of image attributes that our model could use and still get within significance to the full combined model is three – SIFT, RGB Texture, and HOG. However, we found that each image attribute does slightly improve, the model, even if not by a significant amount.

Our results on the handbags category of the dataset are shown in Table 4. Although our scores are not as high as they were in the shoes category, the scores of the corpus frequency baseline are not as high either, and our model does about as well over the baseline in each category. But is worth reiterating that we were able to run our system on both the bags and shoes shopping categories with absolutely no modifications or tuning of parameters.

8 Conclusion and Future Work

In conclusion, we have shown that the polylingual topic model works well for modeling topically comparable images and related text, and obtain competitive results for the image annotation task. Our model is trained on noisy image captions from the web, rather than hand-labeled data.

For future work, we would like to further adapt the polylingual topic model for multi-modal data by allowing some topics to be generated only by one modality or the other. We are also interested in characterizing the image annotations in order to generate a single most likely annotation for different types of features such as texture or color. Finally, we are interested in extending this model to use with other domains of data. For natural images, we could use image segmentation algorithms to separate the object of interest from the background of the image, or we could use scene classifcation to cluster the training images by their background scene and train seprate models for each.

References

K. Barnard, P. Duygulu, D. Forsyth, N. De Freitas, D.M. Blei, and M.I. Jordan. 2003. Matching words and pictures. *The Journal of Machine Learning Research*, 3:1107–1135.

Tamara L. Berg, Alexander C. Berg, and Jonathan Shih. 2010. Automatic attribute discovery and characterization from noisy web data. In *Proceedings of the 11th European conference on Computer vision: Part I*, ECCV'10, pages 663–676, Berlin, Heidelberg. Springer-Verlag.

David M. Blei, Andrew Y. Ng, and Michael I. Jordan. 2003. Latent dirichlet allocation. *J. Mach. Learn. Res.*, 3:993–1022, March.

N. Dalal and B. Triggs. 2005. Histograms of oriented gradients for human detection. In *Computer Vision and Pattern Recognition, 2005. CVPR 2005. IEEE Computer Society Conference on*, volume 1, pages 886 –893 vol. 1, june.

P. F. Felzenszwalb, R. B. Girshick, and D. McAllester. Discriminatively trained deformable part models, release 4. http://people.cs.uchicago.edu/ pff/latent-release4/.

Yansong Feng and Mirella Lapata. 2010a. How many words is a picture worth? automatic caption generation for news images. In *Proceedings of the 48th Annual Meeting of the Association for Computational Linguistics*, ACL '10, pages 1239–1249, Stroudsburg, PA, USA. Association for Computational Linguistics.

Yansong Feng and Mirella Lapata. 2010b. Topic models for image annotation and text illustration. In *HLT-NAACL*, pages 831–839.

Yangqing Jia, M. Salzmann, and T. Darrell. 2011. Learning cross-modality similarity for multinomial data. In *Computer Vision (ICCV), 2011 IEEE International Conference on*, pages 2407 –2414, nov.

T. Leung and J. Malik. 2001. Representing and recognizing the visual appearance of materials using three-dimensional textons. *International Journal of Computer Vision*, 43(1):29–44.

C. Liu, L. Sharan, E.H. Adelson, and R. Rosenholtz. 2010. Exploring features in a bayesian framework for material recognition. In *Computer Vision and Pattern Recognition (CVPR), 2010 IEEE Conference on*, pages 239–246. IEEE.

D.G. Lowe. 1999. Object recognition from local scale-invariant features. In *Computer Vision, 1999. The Proceedings of the Seventh IEEE International Conference on*, volume 2, pages 1150 –1157 vol.2.

R. Mason and E. Charniak. 2012. Apples to oranges: Evaluating image annotations from natural language processing systems. NAACL.

Andrew Kachites McCallum. 2002. Mallet: A machine learning for language toolkit. http://mallet.cs.umass.edu.

David Mimno, Hanna M. Wallach, Jason Naradowsky, David A. Smith, and Andrew McCallum. 2009. Polylingual topic models. In *Proceedings of the 2009 Conference on Empirical Methods in Natural Language Processing: Volume 2 - Volume 2*, EMNLP '09, pages 880–889, Stroudsburg, PA, USA. Association for Computational Linguistics.

Florent Monay and Daniel Gatica-Perez. 2003. On image auto-annotation with latent space models. In *Proceedings of the eleventh ACM international conference on Multimedia*, Multimedia '03, pages 275–278, New York, NY, USA. ACM.

Henning Müller, Stéphane Marchand-Maillet, and Thierry Pun. 2002. The truth about corel - evaluation in image retrieval. In *Proceedings of the International Conference on Image and Video Retrieval*, CIVR '02, pages 38–49, London, UK, UK. Springer-Verlag.

V. Ordonez, G. Kulkarni, and T.L. Berg. 2011. Im2text: Describing images using 1 million captioned photographs. NIPS.

Jeffrey C. Reynar and Adwait Ratnaparkhi. 1997. A maximum entropy approach to identifying sentence boundaries. In *In Proceedings of the Fifth Conference on Applied Natural Language Processing*, pages 16–19.

Kristina Toutanova, Dan Klein, Christopher D. Manning, and Yoram Singer. 2003. Feature-rich part-of-speech tagging with a cyclic dependency network. In *In Proceedings of HLT-NAACL 2003*, pages 252–259.

A. Vedaldi and B. Fulkerson. 2008. VLFeat: An open and portable library of computer vision algorithms. `http://www.vlfeat.org/`.

Generating Natural-Language Video Descriptions Using Text-Mined Knowledge

Niveda Krishnamoorthy *
UT Austin
niveda@cs.utexas.edu

Girish Malkarnenkar *
UT Austin
girish@cs.utexas.edu

Raymond Mooney
UT Austin
mooney@cs.utexas.edu

Kate Saenko
UMass Lowell
saenko@cs.uml.edu

Sergio Guadarrama
UC Berkeley
sguada@eecs.berkeley.edu

Abstract

We present a holistic data-driven technique that generates natural-language descriptions for videos. We combine the output of state-of-the-art object and activity detectors with "real-world" knowledge to select the most probable subject-verb-object triplet for describing a video. We show that this knowledge, automatically mined from web-scale text corpora, enhances the triplet selection algorithm by providing it contextual information and leads to a four-fold increase in activity identification. Unlike previous methods, our approach can annotate arbitrary videos without requiring the expensive collection and annotation of a similar training video corpus. We evaluate our technique against a baseline that does not use text-mined knowledge and show that humans prefer our descriptions 61% of the time.

1 Introduction

Combining natural-language processing (NLP) with computer vision to to generate English descriptions of visual data is an important area of active research (Farhadi et al., 2010; Motwani and Mooney, 2012; Yang et al., 2011). We present a novel approach to generating a simple sentence for describing a short video that:

1. Identifies the most likely subject, verb and object (SVO) using a combination of visual object and activity detectors and text-mined knowledge to judge the likelihood of SVO triplets. From a natural-language generation (NLG) perspective, this is the *content planning* stage.

2. Given the selected SVO triplet, it uses a simple template-based approach to generate candidate sentences which are then ranked using a statistical language model trained on web-scale data to obtain the best overall description. This is the *surface realization* stage.

Figure 1 shows sample system output. Our approach can be viewed as a holistic data-driven three-step process where we first detect objects and activities using state-of-the-art visual recognition algorithms. Next, we combine these often noisy detections with an estimate of real-world likelihood, which we obtain by mining SVO triplets from large-scale web corpora. Finally, these triplets are used to generate candidate sentences which are then ranked for plausibility and grammaticality. The resulting natural-language descriptions can be usefully employed in applications such as semantic video search and summarization, and providing video interpretations for the visually impaired.

Using vision models alone to predict the best subject and object for a given activity is problematic, especially while dealing with challenging real-world YouTube videos as shown in Figures 4 and 5, as it requires a large annotated video corpus of similar SVO triplets (Packer et al., 2012). We are interested in annotating arbitrary short videos using off-the-shelf visual detectors, without the engineering effort required to build domain-specific activity models. Our main contribution is incorporating the pragmatics of various entities' likelihood of being

*Indicates equal contribution

Figure 1: Content planning and surface realization

the subject/object of a given activity, learned from web-scale text corpora. For example, animate objects like people and dogs are more likely to be subjects compared to inanimate objects like balls or TV monitors. Likewise, certain objects are more likely to function as subjects/objects of certain activities, e.g., "riding a horse" vs. "riding a house."

Selecting the best verb may also require recognizing activities for which no explicit training data has been provided. For example, consider a video with a man walking his dog. The object detectors might identify the man and dog; however the action detectors may only have the more general activity, "move," in their training data. In such cases, real-world pragmatics is very helpful in suggesting that "walk" is best used to describe a man "moving" with his dog. We refer to this process as *verb expansion*.

After describing the details of our approach, we present experiments evaluating it on a real-world corpus of YouTube videos. Using a variety of methods for judging the output of the system, we demonstrate that it frequently generates useful descriptions of videos and outperforms a purely vision-based approach that does not utilize text-mined knowledge.

2 Background and Related Work

Although there has been a lot of interesting work done in natural language generation (Bangalore and Rambow, 2000; Langkilde and Knight, 1998), we use a simple template for generating our sentences as we found it to work well for our task.

Most prior work on natural-language description of visual data has focused on static images (Felzenszwalb et al., 2008; Kulkarni et al., 2011; Kuznetsova et al., 2012; Laptev et al., 2008; Li et al., 2011; Yao et al., 2010). The small amount of existing work on videos (Ding et al., 2012; Khan and Gotoh, 2012; Kojima et al., 2002; Lee et al., 2008; Yao and Fei-Fei, 2010) uses hand-crafted templates or rule-based systems, works in constrained domains, and does not exploit text mining. Barbu et al. (2012) produce sentential descriptions for short video clips by using an interesting dynamic programming approach combined with Hidden Markov Models for obtaining verb labels for each video. However, they do not use any text mining to improve the quality of their visual detections.

Our work differs in that we make extensive use of text-mined knowledge to select the best SVO triple and generate coherent sentences. We also evaluate our approach on a generic, large and diverse set of challenging YouTube videos that cover a wide range of activities. Motwani and Mooney (2012) explore how object detection and text mining can aid activity recognition in videos; however, they do not determine a complete SVO triple for describing a video nor generate a full sentential description.

With respect to static image description, Li et al. (2011) generate sentences given visual detections of objects, visual attributes and spatial relationships; however, they do not consider actions. Farhadi et al. (2010) propose a system that maps images and the corresponding textual descriptions to a "meaning" space which consists of an object, action and scene triplet. However, they assume a single object per image and do not use text-mining to determine the likelihood of objects matching different verbs. Yang et al. (2011) is the most similar to our approach in that it uses text-mined knowledge to generate sentential descriptions of static images after performing object and scene detection. However, they do not perform activity recognition nor use text-mining to select the best verb.

3 Approach

Our overall approach is illustrated in Figure 2 and consists of visual object and activity recognition followed by content-planning to generate the best SVO triple and surface realization to generate the final sentence.

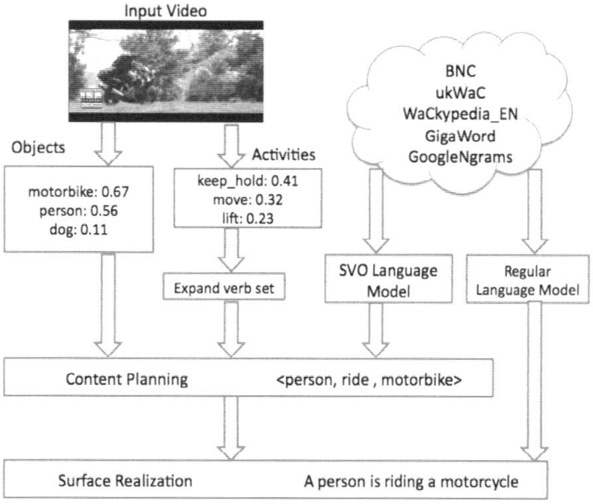

Figure 2: Summary of our approach

Figure 3: Activity clusters discovered by HAC

3.1 Dataset

We used the English portion of the YouTube data collected by Chen et al. (2010), consisting of short videos each with multiple natural-language descriptions. This data was previously used by Motwani and Mooney (2012), and like them, we ensured that the test data only contained videos in which we can potentially detect objects. We used the object detector by Felzenszwalb et al. (2008) as it achieves the state-of-the-art performance on the PASCAL Visual Object Classes (VOC) Challenge. As such, we selected test videos whose subjects and objects belong to the 20 VOC object classes - *aeroplane, car, horse, sheep, bicycle, cat, sofa, bird, chair, motorbike, train, boat, cow, person, tv monitor, bottle, dining table, bus, dog, potted plant*. During this filtering, we also allow synonyms of these object names by including all words with a Lesk similarity (as implemented by Pedersen et al. (2004)) of at least 0.5.[1] Using this approach, we chose 235 potential test videos; the remaining 1,735 videos were reserved for training.

All the published activity recognition methods that work on datasets such as KTH (Schuldt et al., 2004), Drinking and Smoking (Laptev and Perez, 2007) and UCF50 (Reddy and Shah, 2012) have a very limited recognition vocabulary of activity classes. Since we did not have explicit activity labels for our YouTube videos, we followed Motwani and Mooney (2012)'s approach to automatically discover activity clusters. We first parsed the training descriptions using Stanford's dependency parser (De Marneffe et al., 2006) to obtain the set of verbs describing each video. We then clustered these verbs using Hierarchical Agglomerative Clustering (HAC) using the *res* metric from WordNet::Similarity by Pedersen et al. (2004) to measure the distance between verbs. By manually cutting the resulting hierarchy at a desired level (ensuring that each cluster has at least 9 videos), we discovered the 58 activity clusters shown in Figure 3. We then filtered the training and test sets to ensure that all verbs belonged to these 58 activity clusters. The final data contains 185 test and 1,596 training videos.

3.2 Object Detection

We used Felzenszwalb et al. (2008)'s discriminatively-trained deformable parts models to detect the most likely objects in each video. Since these object detectors were designed for static images, each video was split into frames at one-second intervals. For each frame, we ran the object detectors and selected the maximum score assigned to each object in any of the frames. We converted the detection scores, $f(x)$, to estimated probabilities $p(x)$ using a sigmoid $p(x) = \frac{1}{1+e^{-f(x)}}$.

3.3 Activity Recognition

In order to get an initial probability distribution for activities detected in the videos, we used the motion descriptors developed by Laptev et al. (2008). Their approach extracts spatio-temporal interest points (STIPs) from which it computes HoG (Histograms

[1] Empirically, this method worked better than using WordNet synsets.

Corpora	Size of text
British National Corpus (BNC)	1.5GB
WaCkypedia_EN	2.6GB
ukWaC	5.5GB
Gigaword	26GB
GoogleNgrams	10^{12} words

Table 1: Corpora used to Mine SVO Triplets

of Oriented Gradients) and HoF (Histograms of Optical Flow) features over a 3-dimensional space-time volume. These descriptors are then randomly sampled and clustered to obtain a "bag of visual words," and each video is then represented as a histogram over these clusters. We experimented with different classifiers such as LIBSVM (Chang and Lin, 2011) to train a final activity detector using these features. Since we achieved the best classification accuracy (still only 8.65%) using an SVM with the intersection kernel, we used this approach to obtain a probability distribution over the 58 activity clusters for each test video. We later experimented with Dense Trajectories (Wang et al., 2011) for activity recognition but there was only a minor improvement.

3.4 Text Mining

We improve these initial probability distributions over objects and activities by incorporating the likelihood of different activities occuring with particular subjects and objects using two different approaches. In the first approach, using the Stanford dependency parser, we parsed 4 different text corpora covering a wide variety of text: English Gigaword, British National Corpus (BNC), ukWac and WaCkypedia_EN. In order to obtain useful estimates, it is essential to collect text that approximates all of the written language in scale and distribution. The sizes of these corpora (after preprocessing) are shown in Table 1.

Using the dependency parses for these corpora, we mined SVO triplets. Specifically, we looked for subject-verb relationships using *nsubj* dependencies and verb-object relationships using *dobj* and *prep_* dependencies. The *prep_* dependency ensures that we account for intransitive verbs with prepositional objects. Synonyms of subjects and objects and conjugations of verbs were reduced to their base forms (20 object classes, 58 activity clusters) while forming triplets. If a subject, verb or object not belonging to these base forms is encountered, it is ignored during triplet construction.

These triplets are then used to train a backoff language model with Kneser-Ney smoothing (Chen and Goodman, 1999) for estimating the likelihood of an SVO triple. In this model, if we have not seen training data for a particular SVO trigram, we "back-off" to the Subject-Verb and Verb-Object bigrams to coherently estimate its probability. This results in a sophisticated statistical model for estimating triplet probabilities using the syntactic context in which the words have previously occurred. This allows us to effectively determine the real-world plausibility of any SVO using knowledge automatically mined from raw text. We call this the "SVO Language Model" approach (SVO LM).

In a second approach to estimating SVO probabilities, we used BerkeleyLM (Pauls and Klein, 2011) to train an n-gram language model on the GoogleNgram corpus (Lin et al., 2012). This simple model does not consider synonyms, verb conjugations, or SVO dependencies but only looks at word sequences. Given an SVO triplet as an input sequence, it estimates its probability based on n-grams. We refer to this as the "Language Model" approach (LM).

3.5 Verb Expansion

As mentioned earlier, the top activity detections are expanded with their most similar verbs in order to generate a larger set of potential words for describing the action. We used the WUP metric from WordNet::Similarity to expand each activity cluster to include all verbs with a similarity of at least 0.5. For example, we expand the verb "move" with *go 1.0, walk 0.8, pass 0.8, follow 0.8, fly 0.8, fall 0.8, come 0.8, ride 0.8, run 0.67, chase 0.67, approach 0.67*, where the number is the WUP similarity.

3.6 Content Planning

To combine the vision detection and NLP scores and determine the best overall SVO, we use simple linear interpolation as shown in Equation 1. When computing the overall vision score, we make a conditional independence assumption and multiply the probabilities of the subject, activity and object. To account for expanded verbs, we additionally multiply by the WUP similarity between the original

(V_{orig}) and expanded (V_{sim}) verbs. The NLP score is obtained from either the "SVO Language Model" or the "Language Model" approach, as previously described.

$$score = w_1 * vis\_score + w_2 * nlp\_score \quad (1)$$

$$\begin{aligned} vis\_score = P(S|vid) * P(V_{orig}|vid) \\ * Sim(V_{sim}, V_{orig}) * P(O|vid) \end{aligned} \quad (2)$$

After determining the top *n=5* object detections and top *k=10* verb detections for each video, we generate all possible SVO triplets from these nouns and verbs, including all potential verb expansions. Each resulting SVO is then scored using Equation 1, and the best is selected. We compare this approach to a "pure vision" baseline where the subject is the highest scored object detection (which empirically is more likely to be the subject than the object), the object is the second highest scored object detection, and the verb is the activity cluster with the highest detection probability.

3.7 Surface Realization

Finally, the subject, verb and object from the top-scoring SVO are used to produce a set of candidate sentences, which are then ranked using a language model. The text corpora in Table 1 are mined again to get the top three prepositions for every verb-object pair. We use a template-based approach in which each sentence is of the form:

"Determiner (A,The) - Subject - Verb (Present, Present Continuous) - Preposition (optional) - Determiner (A,The) - Object."

Using this template, a set of candidate sentences are generated and ranked using the BerkeleyLM language model trained on the GoogleNgram corpus. The top sentence is then used to describe the video. This surface realization technique is used for both the vision baseline triplet and our proposed triplet.

In addition to the one presented here, we tried alternative "pure vision" baselines, but they are not included since they performed worse. We tried a non-parametric approach similar to Ordonez et al. (2011), which computes global similarity of the query to a large captioned dataset and returns the nearest neighbor's description. To compute the similarity we used an RBF-Chi^2 kernel over bag-of-words STIP features. However, as noted by Ordonez et al. (2011), who used 1 million Flickr images, our dataset is likely not large enough to produce good matches. In an attempt to combine information from both object and activity recognition, we also tried combining object detections from 20 PASCAL object detectors (Felzenszwalb et al., 2008) and from Object Bank (Li et al., 2010) using a multi-channel approach as proposed in (Zhang et al., 2007), with a RBF-Chi^2 kernel for the STIP features and a RBF-Correlation Distance kernel for object detections.

4 Experimental Results

4.1 Content Planning

We first evaluated the ability of the system to identify the best SVO content. From the ~ 50 human descriptions available for each video, we identified the SVO for each description and then determined the ground-truth SVO for each of the 185 test videos using majority vote. These verbs were then mapped back to their 58 activity clusters. For the results presented in Tables 2 and 3, we assigned the vision score a weight of 0 ($w_1 = 0$) and the NLP score a weight of 1 ($w_2 = 1$) since these weights gave us the best performance for thresholds of 5 and 10 for the objects and activity detections respectively. Note that while the vision score is given a weight of zero, the vision detections still play a vital role in the determination of the final triplet since our model only considers the objects and activities with the highest vision detection scores.

To evaluate the accuracy of SVO identification, we used two metrics. The first is a binary metric that requires exactly matching the gold-standard subject, verb and object. We also evaluate the overall triplet accuracy. Note that the verb accuracy in the vision baseline is not word-based and is measured on the 58 activity classes. Its results are shown in Table 2, where VE and NVE stand for "verb expansion" and "no verb expansion" respectively. However, the binary evaluation can be unduly harsh. If we incorrectly choose "bicycle" instead of a "motorbike" as the object, it should be considered better than choosing "dog." Similarly, predicting "chop" instead of "slice" is better than choosing "go".

Method	Subject%	Verb%	Object%	All%
Vision Baseline	71.35	8.65	29.19	1.62
LM(VE)	71.35	8.11	10.81	0.00
SVO LM(NVE)	85.95	16.22	24.32	11.35
SVO LM(VE)	85.95	**36.76**	**33.51**	**23.78**

Table 2: SVO Triplet accuracy: Binary metric

Method	Subject%	Verb%	Object%	All%
Vision Baseline	87.76	40.20	61.18	63.05
LM(VE)	85.77	53.32	61.54	66.88
SVO LM(NVE)	94.90	63.54	69.39	75.94
SVO LM(VE)	94.90	**66.36**	**72.74**	**78.00**

Table 3: SVO Triplet accuracy: WUP metric

In order to account for such similarities, we also measure the WUP similarity between the predicted and correct items. For the examples above, the relevant scores are: *wup(motorbike,bicycle)=0.7826, wup(motorbike,dog)=0.1, wup(slice,chop)=0.8, wup(slice,go)=0.2857.* The results for the WUP metric are shown in Table 3.

4.2 Surface Realization

Figures 4 and 5 show examples of good and bad sentences generated by our method compared to the vision baseline.

4.2.1 Automatic Metrics

To automatically compare the sentences generated for the test videos to ground-truth human descriptions, we employed the BLEU and METEOR metrics used to evaluate machine-translation output. METEOR was designed to fix some of the problems with the more popular BLEU metric. They both measure the number of matching n-grams (for various values of n) between the automatic and human generated sentences. METEOR takes stemming and synonymy into consideration. We used the SVO Language Model (with verb expansion) approach since it gave us the best results for triplets. The results are given in Table 4.

4.2.2 Human Evaluation using Mechanical Turk

Given the limitations of metrics like BLEU and METEOR, we also asked human judges to evaluate the quality of the sentences generated by our ap-

Proposed: A person is riding a motorbike.
Baseline: A person plays a bicycle.
Ground truth: A man is riding a motorcycle.
URL: http://www.youtube.com/watch?v=SPL2sQd65YY

Proposed: A person is riding a horse.
Baseline: A person plays a cat.
Ground truth: A woman is riding on a horse.
URL: http://www.youtube.com/watch?v=X09MVEENMbc

Proposed: A person goes to the car.
Baseline: A person plays a bottle.
Ground truth: A girl is jumping onto a car.
URL: http://www.youtube.com/watch?v=JQevO6OKDVA

Figure 4: Examples where we outperform the baseline

Proposed: A person pulls the chair.
Baseline: A person plays a bottle.
Ground truth: A woman is drinking from a bottle.
URL: http://www.youtube.com/watch?v=Rkail8Oqbis

Proposed: A person is walking a dog.
Baseline: A person plays a cat.
Ground truth: A baby plays with a cat.
URL: http://www.youtube.com/watch?v=YIUCwNsMIHM

Proposed: A person rides a car.
Baseline: A person moves a cat.
Ground truth: A man is dragging a cat.
URL: http://www.youtube.com/watch?v=NOGAlpPXd4o

Figure 5: Examples where we underperform the baseline

proach compared to those generated by the baseline system. For each of the 185 test videos, we asked 9 unique workers (with >95% HIT approval rate and who had worked on more than 1000 HITs) on Amazon Mechanical Turk to pick which sentence better described the video. We also gave them a "none of the above two sentences" option in case neither of the sentences were relevant to the video. Quality was controlled by also including in each HIT a gold-standard example generated from the human descriptions, and discarding judgements of workers who incorrectly answered this gold-standard item. Overall, when they expressed a preference, humans picked our descriptions to that of the baseline

Method	BLEU score	METEOR score
Vision Baseline	0.37±0.05	0.25±0.08
SVO LM(VE)	0.45±0.05	0.36±0.27

Table 4: Automatic evaluation of sentence quality

61.04% of the time. Out of the 84 videos where the majority of judges had a clear preference, they chose our descriptions **65.48%** of the time.

5 Discussion

Overall, the results consistently show the advantage of utilizing text-mined knowledge to improve the selection of an SVO that best describes a video. Below we discuss various specific aspects of the results.

Vision Baseline: For the vision baseline, the subject accuracy is quite high compared to the object and activity accuracies. This is likely because the person detector has higher recall and confidence than the other object detectors. Since most test videos have a person as the subject, this works in favor of the vision baseline, as typically the top object detection is "person". Activity (verb) accuracy is quite low (8.65% binary accuracy). This is because there are 58 activity clusters, some with very little training data. Object accuracy is not as high as subject accuracy because the true object, while usually present in the top object detections, is not always the second-highest object detection. By allowing "partial credit", the WUP metric increases the verb and object accuracies to 40.2% and 61.18%, respectively.

Language Model(VE): The Language Model approach performs even worse than the vision baseline especially for object identification. This is because we consider the language model score directly for the SVO triplet without any verb conjugations and presence of determiners between the verb and object. For example, while the GoogleNgram corpus is likely to contain many instances of a sentence like "A person is walking with a dog", it will probably not contain many instances of "person walk dog", resulting in lower scores.

SVO Language Model(NVE): The SVO Language Model (without verb expansion) improves verb accuracy from 8.65% to 16.22%. For the WUP metric, we see an improvement in accuracy in all cases. This indicates that we are getting semantically closer to the right object compared to the object predicted by the vision baseline.

SVO Language Model(VE): When used with verb expansion, the SVO Language Model approach results in a dramatic improvement in verb accuracy, causing it to jump to 36.76%. The WUP score increase for verbs between SVO Language Model(VE) and SVO Language Model(NVE) is minor, probably because even without verb expansion, semantically similar verbs are selected but not the one used in most human descriptions. So, the jump in verb accuracy for the binary metric is much more than the one for WUP.

Importance of verb expansion: Verb expansion clearly improves activity accuracy. This idea could be extended to a scenario where the test set contains many activities for which we do not have any explicit training data. As such, we cannot train activity classifiers for these "missing" classes. However, we can train a "coarse" activity classifier using the training data that is available, get the top predictions from this coarse classifier and then refine them by using verb expansion. Thus, we can even detect and describe activities that were unseen at training time by using text-mined knowledge to determine the description of an activity that best fits the detected objects.

Effect of different training corpora: As mentioned earlier, we used a variety of textual corpora. Since they cover newswire articles, web pages, Wikipedia pages and neutral content, we compared their individual effect on the accuracy of triplet selection. The results of this ablation study are shown in Tables 5 and 6 for the binary and WUP metric respectively. We also show results for training the SVO model on the descriptions of the training videos. The WaCkypedia_EN corpus gives us the best overall results, probably because it covers a wide variety of topics, unlike Gigaword which is restricted to the news domain. Also, using our SVO Language Model approach on the triplets from the descriptions of the training videos is not sufficient. This is because of the relatively small size and narrow domain of the training descriptions in comparison to the other textual corpora.

Effect of changing the weight of the NLP score We experimented with different weights for the Vision and NLP scores (in Equation 1). These results can be seen in Figure 6 for the binary-metric evaluation. The WUP-metric evaluation graph is qualitatively similar. A general trend seems to be that the subject and activity accuracies increase with increasing weights of the NLP score. There is a significant

Method	Subject%	Verb%	Object%	All%
Vision Baseline	71.35	8.65	29.19	1.62
Train Desc.	**85.95**	16.22	16.22	8.65
Gigaword	**85.95**	32.43	20.00	14.05
BNC	**85.95**	17.30	29.73	14.59
ukWaC	**85.95**	34.05	32.97	22.16
WaCkypedia_EN	**85.95**	35.14	**40.00**	**28.11**
All	**85.95**	**36.76**	33.51	23.78

Table 5: Effect of training corpus on SVO binary accuracy

Method	Subject%	Verb%	Object%	All%
Vision Baseline	87.76	40.20	61.18	63.05
Train Desc.	**94.95**	45.12	61.43	67.17
Gigaword	94.90	63.99	65.71	74.87
BNC	94.88	51.48	73.93	73.43
ukWaC	94.86	60.59	72.83	76.09
WaCkypedia_EN	94.90	62.52	**76.48**	77.97
All	94.90	**66.36**	72.74	**78.00**

Table 6: Effect of training corpus on SVO WUP accuracy

improvement in verb accuracy as the NLP weight is increased towards 1. However, for objects we notice a slight increase in accuracy until the weight for the NLP component is 0.9 after which there is a slight dip. We hypothesize that this dip is caused by the loss of vision-based information about the objects which provide some guidance for the NLP system.

BLEU and METEOR results: From the results in Table 4, it is clear that the sentences generated by our approach outperform those generated by the vision baseline, using both the BLEU and METEOR evaluation metrics.

MTurk results: The Mechanical Turk results show that human judges generally prefer our system's sentences to those of the vision baseline. As previously seen, our method improves verbs far more than it improves subjects or objects. We hypothesize that the reason we do not achieve a similarly large jump in performance in the MTurk evaluation is because people seem to be more influenced by the object than the verb when both options are partially irrelevant. For example, in a video of a person riding his bike onto the top of a car, our proposed sentence was "A person is a riding a motorbike" while the vision sentence was "A person plays

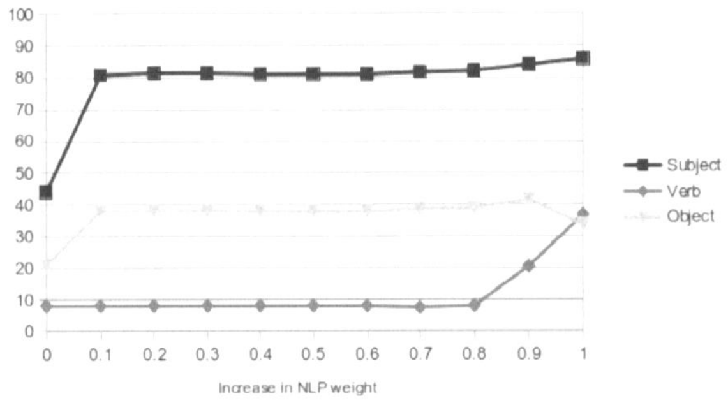

Figure 6: Effect of increasing NLP weights (Binary metric)

a car", and most workers selected the vision sentence.

Drawback of Using YouTube Videos: YouTube videos often depict unusual and "interesting" events, and these might not agree with the statistics on typical SVOs mined from text corpora. For instance, the last video in Figure 5 shows a person dragging a cat on the floor. Since sentences describing people moving or dragging cats around are not common in text corpora, our system actually down-weights the correct interpretation.

6 Conclusion

This paper has introduced a holistic data-driven approach for generating natural-language descriptions of short videos by identifying the best subject-verb-object triplet for describing realistic YouTube videos. By exploiting knowledge mined from large corpora to determine the likelihood of various SVO combinations, we improve the ability to select the best triplet for describing a video and generate descriptive sentences that are prefered by both automatic and human evaluation. From our experiments, we see that linguistic knowledge significantly improves activity detection, especially when training and test distributions are very different, one of the advantages of our approach. Generating more complex sentences with adjectives, adverbs, and multiple objects and multi-sentential descriptions of longer videos with multiple activities are areas for future research.

7 Acknowledgements

This work was funded by NSF grant IIS1016312 and DARPA Minds Eye grant W911NF-10-2-0059. Some of our experiments were run on the Mastodon Cluster (NSF Grant EIA-0303609).

References

Bangalore, S. and Rambow, O. (2000), Exploiting a probabilistic hierarchical model for generation, *in* 'Proceedings of the 18th conference on Computational linguistics-Volume 1', Association for Computational Linguistics, pp. 42–48.

Barbu, A., Bridge, A., Burchill, Z., Coroian, D., Dickinson, S., Fidler, S., Michaux, A., Mussman, S., Narayanaswamy, S., Salvi, D. et al. (2012), Video in sentences out, *in* 'Proceedings of the 28th Conference on Uncertainty in Artificial Intelligence (UAI)', pp. 102–12.

Chang, C. and Lin, C. (2011), 'LIBSVM: a library for support vector machines', *ACM Transactions on Intelligent Systems and Technology (TIST)* **2**(3), 27.

Chen, D., Dolan, W., Raghavan, S., Huynh, T., Mooney, R., Blythe, J., Hobbs, J., Domingos, P., Kate, R., Garrette, D. et al. (2010), 'Collecting highly parallel data for paraphrase evaluation', *Journal of Artificial Intelligence Research (JAIR)* **37**, 397–435.

Chen, S. and Goodman, J. (1999), 'An empirical study of smoothing techniques for language modeling', *Computer Speech & Language* **13**(4), 359–393.

De Marneffe, M., MacCartney, B. and Manning, C. (2006), Generating typed dependency parses from phrase structure parses, *in* 'Proceedings of the International Conference on Language Resources and Evaluation (LREC)', Vol. 6, pp. 449–454.

Ding, D., Metze, F., Rawat, S., Schulam, P., Burger, S., Younessian, E., Bao, L., Christel, M. and Hauptmann, A. (2012), Beyond audio and video retrieval: towards multimedia summarization, *in* 'Proceedings of the 2nd ACM International Conference on Multimedia Retrieval'.

Farhadi, A., Hejrati, M., Sadeghi, M., Young, P., Rashtchian, C., Hockenmaier, J. and Forsyth, D. (2010), 'Every picture tells a story: Generating sentences from images', *Computer Vision–European Conference on Computer Vision (ECCV)* pp. 15–29.

Felzenszwalb, P., McAllester, D. and Ramanan, D. (2008), A discriminatively trained, multiscale, deformable part model, *in* 'IEEE Conference on Computer Vision and Pattern Recognition (CVPR)', pp. 1–8.

Khan, M. and Gotoh, Y. (2012), 'Describing video contents in natural language', *European Chapter of the Association for Computational Linguistics (EACL)* .

Kojima, A., Tamura, T. and Fukunaga, K. (2002), 'Natural language description of human activities from video images based on concept hierarchy of actions', *International Journal of Computer Vision (IJCV)* **50**(2), 171–184.

Kulkarni, G., Premraj, V., Dhar, S., Li, S., Choi, Y., Berg, A. and Berg, T. (2011), Baby talk: Understanding and generating simple image descriptions, *in* 'IEEE Conference on Computer Vision and Pattern Recognition (CVPR)', pp. 1601–1608.

Kuznetsova, P., Ordonez, V., Berg, A. C., Berg, T. L. and Choi, Y. (2012), Collective generation of natural image descriptions, *in* 'Proceedings of the 50th Annual Meeting of the Association for Computational Linguistics: Long Papers-Volume 1', Association for Computational Linguistics, pp. 359–368.

Langkilde, I. and Knight, K. (1998), Generation that exploits corpus-based statistical knowledge, *in* 'Proceedings of the 17th international conference on Computational linguistics-Volume 1', Association for Computational Linguistics, pp. 704–710.

Laptev, I., Marszalek, M., Schmid, C. and Rozenfeld, B. (2008), Learning realistic human actions from movies, *in* 'IEEE Conference on Computer Vision and Pattern Recognition (CVPR)', pp. 1–8.

Laptev, I. and Perez, P. (2007), Retrieving actions in movies, *in* 'Proceedings of the 11th IEEE International Conference on Computer Vision (ICCV)', pp. 1–8.

Lee, M., Hakeem, A., Haering, N. and Zhu, S.

(2008), Save: A framework for semantic annotation of visual events, *in* 'IEEE Computer Vision and Pattern Recognition Workshops (CVPR-W)', pp. 1–8.

Li, L., Su, H., Xing, E. and Fei-Fei, L. (2010), 'Object bank: A high-level image representation for scene classification and semantic feature sparsification', *Advances in Neural Information Processing Systems (NIPS)* **24**.

Li, S., Kulkarni, G., Berg, T., Berg, A. and Choi, Y. (2011), Composing simple image descriptions using web-scale n-grams, *in* 'Proceedings of the Fifteenth Conference on Computational Natural Language Learning (CoNLL)', Association for Computational Linguistics (ACL), pp. 220–228.

Lin, Y., Michel, J., Aiden, E., Orwant, J., Brockman, W. and Petrov, S. (2012), Syntactic annotations for the google books ngram corpus, *in* 'Proceedings of the 50th Annual Meeting of the Association for Computational Linguistics (ACL)'.

Motwani, T. and Mooney, R. (2012), Improving video activity recognition using object recognition and text mining, *in* 'European Conference on Artificial Intelligence (ECAI)'.

Ordonez, V., Kulkarni, G. and Berg, T. (2011), Im2text: Describing images using 1 million captioned photographs, *in* 'Proceedings of Advances in Neural Information Processing Systems (NIPS)'.

Packer, B., Saenko, K. and Koller, D. (2012), A combined pose, object, and feature model for action understanding, *in* 'IEEE Conference on Computer Vision and Pattern Recognition (CVPR)', pp. 1378–1385.

Pauls, A. and Klein, D. (2011), Faster and smaller n-gram language models, *in* 'Proceedings of the 49th annual meeting of the Association for Computational Linguistics: Human Language Technologies', Vol. 1, pp. 258–267.

Pedersen, T., Patwardhan, S. and Michelizzi, J. (2004), Wordnet:: Similarity: measuring the relatedness of concepts, *in* 'Demonstration Papers at Human Language Technologies-NAACL', Association for Computational Linguistics, pp. 38–41.

Reddy, K. and Shah, M. (2012), 'Recognizing 50 human action categories of web videos', *Machine Vision and Applications* pp. 1–11.

Schuldt, C., Laptev, I. and Caputo, B. (2004), Recognizing human actions: A local SVM approach, *in* 'Proceedings of the 17th International Conference on Pattern Recognition (ICPR)', Vol. 3, pp. 32–36.

Wang, H., Klaser, A., Schmid, C. and Liu, C.-L. (2011), Action recognition by dense trajectories, *in* 'IEEE Conference on Computer Vision and Pattern Recognition (CVPR)', pp. 3169–3176.

Yang, Y., Teo, C. L., Daumé, III, H. and Aloimonos, Y. (2011), Corpus-guided sentence generation of natural images, *in* 'Proceedings of the Conference on Empirical Methods in Natural Language Processing (EMNLP)', Association for Computational Linguistics, pp. 444–454.

Yao, B. and Fei-Fei, L. (2010), Modeling mutual context of object and human pose in human-object interaction activities, *in* 'IEEE Conference on Computer Vision and Pattern Recognition (CVPR)'.

Yao, B., Yang, X., Lin, L., Lee, M. and Zhu, S. (2010), 'I2t: Image parsing to text description', *Proceedings of the IEEE* **98**(8), 1485–1508.

Zhang, J., Marszałek, M., Lazebnik, S. and Schmid, C. (2007), 'Local features and kernels for classification of texture and object categories: A comprehensive study', *International Journal of Computer Vision (IJCV)* **73**(2), 213–238.

Learning Hierarchical Linguistic Descriptions of Visual Datasets

Roni Mittelman[†], **Min Sun**[‡], **Benjamin Kuipers**[†], **Silvio Savarese**[†]
† Department of Electrical Engineering and Computer Science, University of Michigan, Ann Arbor
‡ Department of Computer Science and Engineering, University of Washington, Seatle
`rmittelm,kuipers,silvio@umich.edu, sunmin@cs.washington.edu`

Abstract

We propose a method to learn succinct hierarchical linguistic descriptions of visual datasets, which allow for improved navigation efficiency in image collections. Classic exploratory data analysis methods, such as agglomerative hierarchical clustering, only provide a means of obtaining a tree-structured partitioning of the data. This requires the user to go through the images first, in order to reveal the semantic relationship between the different nodes. On the other hand, in this work we propose to learn a hierarchy of linguistic descriptions, referred to as attributes, which allows for a textual description of the semantic content that is captured by the hierarchy. Our approach is based on a generative model, which relates the attribute descriptions associated with each node, and the node assignments of the data instances, in a probabilistic fashion. We furthermore use a nonparametric Bayesian prior, known as the tree-structured stick breaking process, which allows for the structure of the tree to be learned in an unsupervised fashion. We also propose appropriate performance measures, and demonstrate superior performance compared to other hierarchical clustering algorithms.

1 Introduction

With the abundance of images available both for personal use and in large internet based datasets, such as Flickr and Google Image Search, hierarchies of images are an important tool that allows for convenient browsing and efficient search and retrieval. Intuitively, desirable hierarchies should capture similarity in a semantic space, i.e. nearby nodes should include categories which are semantically more similar, as compared to nodes which are more distant. Recent works that are concerned with learning image hierarchies (Bart et al., 2011; Sivic et al., 2008), have relied on a bag of visual-words feature space, and therefore have been shown to provide unsatisfactory results with respect to the latter requirement (Li et al., 2010).

A recent trend in visual recognition systems, has been to shift from using a low-level feature based representation to an attribute based feature space, which can capture higher level semantics (Farhadi et al., 2009; Lampert et al., 2009; Parikh & Grauman, 2011; Berg et al., 2011; Ferrari & Zisserman, 2007). Attributes are detectors that are trained using annotation data, to identify particular properties in an instance image. By evaluating these detectors on a query image, one can obtain a linguistic description of the image. Therefore, learning a visual hierarchy based on an attribute representation can allow for an improved semantic grouping, as compared to the previous use of low-level image features.

In this work we wish to utilize an attribute based representation to learn a hierarchical linguistic description of a visual dataset, in which few attributes are associated with each node of the tree. As is illustrated in Figure 1, such an attribute hierarchy is tightly related to a category hierarchy, in which the instances associated with every node are described using all the attributes associated with all the nodes along the path leading up to the root node (the instances in Figure 1 are described by the corresponding photographs). This "duality" between the at-

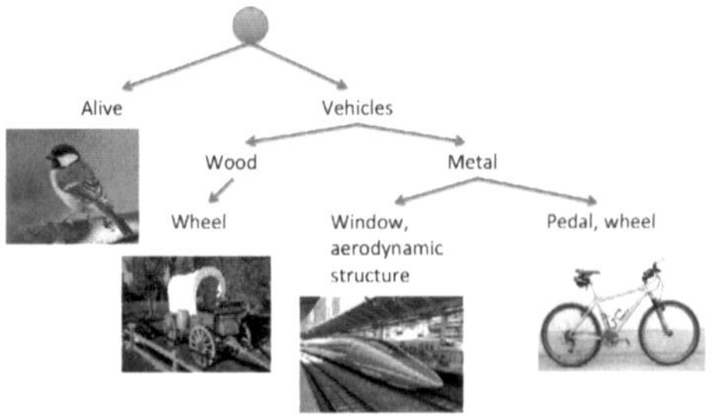

Figure 1: Attribute and category hierarchies.

tribute and category hierarchies, offers an important advantage when characterizing the dataset to the end-user, since it eliminates the need to visually inspect the images assigned to each node, in order to reveal the semantic relationship between the categories that are associated with the different nodes. Exploratory data analysis methods for learning hierarchies, such as agglomerative hierarchical clustering (AHC) (Jain & Dubes, 1988 p. 59), only assign instances to different nodes in the tree, whereas our approach learns an attribute hierarchy which is used to assign the instances to the nodes of the tree. The attribute hierarchy provides a linguistic description of a category hierarchy.

We develop a generative model, which we refer to as the attribute tree process (ATP), and which ties together the attribute and category hierarchies in a probabilistic fashion. The tree structure is learned by incorporating a nonparametric Bayesian prior, known as the tree-structured stick breaking process (TSSBP) (Adams et al., 2010), in the probabilistic formulation. An important observation which we make about the attribute hierarchies which are learned using the ATP, is that attributes which are related to more image instances tend to be associated with nodes which are closer to the root, and vice versa, attributes which are associated with fewer instances tend to be associated with leaf nodes. A hierarchical clustering algorithm that is based on the TSSBP for binary feature vectors was developed in (Adams et al., 2010), and is known as the factored Bernoulli likelihood model (FBLM). However, similarly to AHC, it does not produce the attribute hierarchy in which we are interested.

In order to evaluate the ATP quantitatively, we compare its performance to other hierarchical clustering algorithms. If the ground truth of the category hierarchy is available, we propose to use the semantic distance between the categories, that is given by the ground truth hierarchy, to evaluate the degree to which the semantic distance between the categories is preserved by the hierarchical clustering algorithm. If the ground truth is not available, we use two criteria, which as we argue, capture the properties that should be demonstrated by desirable semantic hierarchies. The first is the "purity criterion" (Manning et al., 2009 p. 357) which measures the degree to which each node is occupied by instances from a single class, and the second is the "locality criterion" which we propose, and which measures the degree to which instances from the same class are assigned to nearby nodes in the hierarchy. Our experimental results show that when compared to AHC and FBLM, our approach captures the ground truth semantic distance between the categories more accurately, and without significant dependence on hyperparameters.

The remaining of this paper is organized as follows. In Sec. 2 we provide background on agglomerative hierarchical clustering, and on the TSSBP, and in Sec. 3 we develop the generative model for the ATP. In Sec. 4 we propose evaluation metrics for the attribute hierarchy, and in Sec. 5 we present the experimental results. Sec. 6 concludes this paper.

2 Background

2.1 Agglomerative hierarchical clustering

AHC uses a bottom up approach to clustering. In the first iteration, each cluster includes a single instance of the dataset, and at each following iteration, the two clusters which are closest to each other are joined into a single cluster. This requires a distance metric, which measures the distance between clusters, to be defined. The algorithm concludes when the distance between the farthest clusters is smaller than some threshold.

2.2 Tree structured stick breaking process

The TSSBP is an infinite mixture model, where each mixture component has one-to-one correspondence with one of the nodes of an infinitely branching and infinitely deep tree. The weights of the infinite mixture model are generated by interleaving two stick-breaking processes (Teh et al., 2006), which allows the number of mixture components to be inferred

(a) TSSBP (b) ATP

Figure 2: The graphical model representations of the probability distribution functions for the (a) TSSBP, and (b) ATP (ours). The parameter θ_ϵ is associated with node ϵ in the tree, and T denotes the parameters $\{\pi_\epsilon\}_{\epsilon \in \mathcal{T}}$ from the TSSBP construction, where $\mathcal{T}$ is the set of all the nodes in the tree.

from the data in a Bayesian fashion. Since each mixture component is associated with a unique node in the infinite tree, this is equivalent to inferring the structure of the tree from the data. Let $\mathcal{T}$ denote the infinite set of node indices, and let π_ϵ denote the corresponding weight of the mixture component associated with node $\epsilon \in \mathcal{T}$, then one can sample a node z in the tree using

$$z \sim \sum_{\epsilon \in \mathcal{T}} \pi_\epsilon \delta_\epsilon(z), \tag{1}$$

where $\delta_\epsilon()$ denotes a Dirac delta function at ϵ.

Since the cardinality of the set $\mathcal{T}$ is unbounded, sampling from (1) is not trivial, however, an efficient sampling scheme was presented in (Adams et al., 2010). Similarly, an efficient scheme for sampling from the posterior of $\{\pi_\epsilon\}_{\epsilon \in \mathcal{T}}$ given the node assignments of all the data instances, was also developed in (Adams et al., 2010).

2.2.1 Factored Bernoulli likelihood model

The FBLM was used in (Adams et al., 2010) to perform hierarchical clustering of color images using binary feature vectors. Let $\mathrm{x}_i \in \{0,1\}^D$, $i = 1, \ldots, N$, denote a set of binary training vectors that are available for learning the hierarchy. The graphical model representation of the probability distribution function is shown in Figure 2a, where for the sake of clarity of the exposition, the tree that is shown here is finite. The parameters $\theta_\epsilon = [\theta_\epsilon^{(1)}, \ldots, \theta_\epsilon^{(D)}]^T$ satisfy

$$\theta_\epsilon^{(d)} = \theta_{\mathrm{Pa}(\epsilon)}^{(d)} + n_\epsilon^{(d)},\ d = 1, \ldots, D, \tag{2}$$

where $n_\epsilon^{(d)} \sim \mathcal{N}(0, \sigma^2)$, and $\mathrm{Pa}(\epsilon)$ denotes the parent of node ϵ. The indicator variable z is sampled using (1), and the likelihood of a binary observation vector $\mathrm{x} = [x^{(1)}, \ldots, x^{(D)}]^T$ follows a Bernoulli distribution whose parameter is a logistic function

$$f(\mathrm{x}|\theta_z) = \prod_{d=1}^{D} (1+\exp\{-\theta_z^{(d)}\})^{-x^{(d)}} \times (1+\exp\{\theta_z^{(d)}\})^{-(1-x^{(d)})}. \tag{3}$$

3 The attribute tree process

In this section, we develop a new generative model that is based on the TSSBP, however unlike the FBLM it also reveals a hierarchy of attributes, which allows for a linguistic description of the image dataset. This is achieved by relating the attribute hierarchy, and the assignment of image instances to nodes, in a probabilistic manner.

3.1 The attribute hierarchy

In order to allow for a probabilistic description of the attribute hierarchy, we associate a parameter vector $\theta = [\theta_\epsilon^{(1)}, \ldots, \theta_\epsilon^{(D)}]^T$ with each node $\epsilon \in \mathcal{T}$, where D denotes the number of attributes. The attributes $y_i^{(d)}$, $d = 1, \ldots, D$ that are associated with a data instance i that is assigned to node ϵ, are generated using the following scheme:

1. For each $\epsilon' \in \mathrm{A}(\epsilon)$, draw $\xi_{\epsilon',i}^{(d)} \sim \mathrm{Bernoulli}(\theta_{\epsilon'}^{(d)})$, $d = 1, \ldots, D$,
2. Set $y_i^{(d)} = \bigoplus_{\epsilon' \in \mathrm{A}(\epsilon)} \xi_{\epsilon',i}^{(d)}$, $d = 1, \ldots, D$,

where $\xi_{\epsilon',i}^{(d)}$ is an auxiliary random variable, $\bigoplus$ denotes the logical or operation, and $\mathrm{A}(\epsilon)$ denotes the set composed of all the ancestors of node ϵ. By marginalizing with respect to $\xi_{\epsilon',i}^{(d)}$, we obtain a simplified representation: first set

$h_\epsilon^{(d)} = 1 - \prod_{\epsilon' \in \mathrm{A}(\epsilon)}(1 - \theta_{\epsilon'}^{(d)})$, and then sample $y_i^{(d)} \sim \mathrm{Bernoulli}(h_\epsilon^{(d)})$ for every $d = 1, \ldots, D$.

We use the parameters $h_\epsilon^{(d)}$ to define the attribute hierarchy, since they represent the probability of an attribute being associated with an instance assigned to node ϵ. Furthermore, they satisfy the property that the likelihood of any attribute can only increase when moving deeper into the tree. We can obtain an attribute hierarchy, similar to that in Figure 1, by thresholding $h_\epsilon^{(d)}$, and only displaying attributes that have not been detected at any ancestor node.

In order to complete our probabilistic formulation for the attribute hierarchy, we need to specify the prior for the node parameters θ_ϵ. We use a finite approximation to a hierarchical Beta process (Thibaux & Jordan, 2007; Paisley & Carin, 2009). This choice promotes sparsity, and therefore only few attributes will be associated with each node. Specifically, the parameters at the root node follow

$$\theta_0^{(d)} \sim \mathrm{Beta}(a/D, b(D-1)/D),\ d = 1, \ldots, D, \tag{4}$$

and the parameters in the other nodes follow

$$\theta_\epsilon^{(d)} \sim \mathrm{Beta}(c^{(d)}\theta_{\mathrm{Pa}(\epsilon)}^{(d)}, c^{(d)}(1-\theta_{\mathrm{Pa}(\epsilon)}^{(d)})),\ d = 1, \ldots, D, \tag{5}$$

where $\mathrm{Pa}(\epsilon)$ denotes the parent of node ϵ, and where a, b, and $c^{(d)}$, $d = 1, \ldots, D$ are positive scalar parameters.

In this work we used a uniform prior for the precision hyper-parameter $c^{(d)} \sim U[l, u]$ with $\ell = 20$, and $u = 100$. We also used the hyper-parameter values $a = 10$, and $b = 5$ (unless otherwise stated). In Section 5.1.1 we demonstrate that the performance of our algorithm depends only weakly on the choice of these parameters.

3.2 Assigning images to nodes

In order to assign every image instance to one of the nodes, we combine the attribute hierarchy with the TSSBP. The resulting graphical model representation of the probability distribution function is shown in Figure 2b. For every data instance i, a node z_i in the tree is sampled from the TSSBP. The observed attribute vector x_i is obtained by sampling $y_i^{(d)} \sim \mathrm{Bernoulli}(h_{z_i}^{(d)})$, and flipping $y_i^{(d)}$ with probability ω, which models the effect of the noisy attribute detectors. By marginalizing over $y_i^{(d)}$, we have that

$$p(x_i^{(d)} = 1|-) = 1 - ((1 - h_{z_i}^{(d)})(1 - \omega^{(d)}). + h_{z_i}^{(d)}\omega^{(d)}). \tag{6}$$

The prior for ω is $\omega \sim \mathrm{Beta}(\rho_0, \rho_1)$, where in this work we used $\rho_0 = 5$, and $\rho_1 = 20$, which promotes smaller values for ω. Our algorithm is highly insensitive to the choice of ρ_0, ρ_1, as long as they are chosen to promote small values of ω.

3.3 Inference

Inference in the ATP is based on Gibbs sampling scheme. In order to sample from the posterior of the node parameter $\theta_\epsilon^{(d)}$, we note that

$$\begin{aligned} p(\theta_\epsilon^{(d)}|-) \propto & \\ \prod_{\epsilon' \in \epsilon \cup \mathrm{D}(\epsilon)} & (1 - ((1 - h_{\epsilon'}^{(d)})(1 - \omega^{(d)}) + h_{\epsilon'}^{(d)}\omega^{(d)}))^{n_{\epsilon'}^{(1,d)}} \\ \times & ((1 - h_{\epsilon'}^{(d)})(1 - \omega^{(d)}) + h_{\epsilon'}^{(d)}\omega^{(d)})^{n_{\epsilon'}^{(0,d)}} \\ \times & \prod_{\epsilon'' \in \mathrm{Ch}(\epsilon)} \mathrm{Beta}(\theta_{\epsilon''}^{(d)}; c^{(d)}\theta_\epsilon^{(d)}, c^{(d)}(1 - \theta_\epsilon^{(d)})) \\ \times & \mathrm{Beta}(\theta_\epsilon^{(d)}; a_\epsilon^{(d)}, b_\epsilon^{(d)}), \end{aligned} \tag{7}$$

where $n_\epsilon^{(j,d)} = \sum_{i|z_i=\epsilon} \delta_j(x_i^{(d)})$ for $j = 0, 1$, $\mathrm{D}(\epsilon)$ denotes the set composed of all the descendants of node ϵ, $\mathrm{Ch}(\epsilon)$ denotes the child nodes of node ϵ, and $a_\epsilon^{(d)} = a/D$, $b_\epsilon^{(d)} = b(D-1)/D$, for $\epsilon = 0$ (the root node), and for any other node: $a_\epsilon^{(d)} = c^{(d)}\theta_\epsilon^{(d)}$, $b_\epsilon^{(d)} = c^{(d)}(1 - \theta_\epsilon^{(d)})$. The expression in (7) is a highly complicated function of $\theta_\epsilon^{(d)}$, and therefore we use slice-sampling (Neal, 2000) in order to sample from the posterior. The slice-sampler is very much a "black-box" algorithm, which only requires the log likelihood of (7) and very few parameters, and returns a sample from the posterior. We sample the node parameters using a two-pass approach, starting from the leaf nodes and moving up to the root, and subsequently moving down the tree from the root to the leaves.

In order to sample from ω, we first sample the binary random variables $y_i^{(d)}$ using

$$p(y_i^{(d)} = j|-) \propto p(y_i^{(d)} = j|-)(\delta_j(x_i^{(d)})(1 - \omega^{(d)}) + \delta_{1-j}(x_i^{(d)})\omega^{(d)}),\ j = 0, 1, \tag{8}$$

and then sample ω using

$$\omega^{(d)}|- \sim \text{Beta}\big(\rho_0 + \sum_{i=1}^{N} \delta_1(y_i^{(d)} \text{xor } x_i^{(d)}),$$
$$\rho_1 + \sum_{i=1}^{N} \delta_0(y_i^{(d)} \text{xor } x_i^{(d)})\big). \qquad (9)$$

Sampling from the posterior of the hyper-parameter $c^{(d)}$ was also performed using slice sampling. We note that slice sampling each of the parameters $\theta_\epsilon^{(d)}$ for $d = 1, \ldots, D$, and each of $c^{(d)}$ for $d = 1, \ldots, D$, can be implemented in a parallel fashion. Therefore, the computational bottleneck in the ATP is the number of nodes in the tree, rather than the number of attributes. Sampling from the posterior of the TSSBP parameters is performed using the algorithms developed in (Adams et al., 2010). The parameters of the stick-breaking processes involved in the TSSBP construction are also learned from the data using slice-sampling, by assuming a uniform prior on some interval (as was also performed in (Adams et al., 2010)).

4 Evaluating the attribute hierarchy

In order to quantify the performance of the attribute hierarchies, we evaluate the performance of the ATP as a hierarchical clustering algorithm. We consider two cases, in the first, the ground truth category hierarchy is available and can be used to compare different hierarchies quantitatively. In the second case, the ground truth is unavailable.

4.1 Using the ground truth category hierarchy

The category hierarchy should capture the distance between the categories in a semantic space. For instance, since car and bus are both vehicles, they should be assigned to nodes which are closer, compared to the categories car and sheep, which are semantically less similar. Given the ground truth category hierarchy, we can "measure" the semantic distance between different categories by counting the number of edges that separate any two categories in the graph.

In order to compare the hierarchies learned using different hierarchical clustering algorithms, we propose a criterion which measures the degree to which the semantic distance which a hierarchy assigns to different image instances, diverges from the semantic distance that is given by the ground truth category hierarchy. Let $d_{GT}(c_1, c_2)$ denote the number of edges separating categories c_1 and c_2 in the ground truth category hierarchy, and let $d_H(i, j)$ denote the number of edges separating instances i and j in a hierarchy that is learned using a hierarchical clustering algorithm. Our proposed criterion, which we refer to as the average edge error (AEE), takes the form

$$\frac{2}{N(N-1)} \sum_{i=1}^{N-1} \sum_{j=i+1}^{N} |d_H(i,j) - d_{GT}(c(i), c(j))|, \qquad (10)$$

where $c(i)$ denotes the category of instance i, and N denotes the number of image instances.

4.2 Without ground truth hierarchy

When the ground truth of the category is unavailable, we propose to use the following two criteria in order to evaluate the hierarchies. The first is known as the purity criterion (Manning et al., 2009 p. 357), and the second is the locality criterion which we propose. The purity criterion measures the degree to which each node is occupied by instances from a single class, and takes the form

$$\text{Purity} = \frac{1}{N} \sum_{\epsilon \in \mathcal{T}} \sum_{i=1}^{N_\epsilon} \delta_{c_\epsilon^*}(c(i)), \qquad (11)$$

where N_ϵ denotes the number of instances in node ϵ, and c_ϵ^* is the class which is most frequent in node ϵ.

The locality criterion measures the degree to which each class is concentrated in few adjacent nodes. Quantitatively we define the category locality for class c as

$$\text{CL}_c = -\frac{2}{(|C|-1)|C|} \sum_{\substack{i, j \in C, \\ i \neq j}} \text{dist}(\epsilon_i, \epsilon_j), \qquad (12)$$

where $|\cdot|$ denotes the cardinality of a set, $C = \{i|c_i = c\}$ where c_i is the class associated with instance i, and $\text{dist}(\epsilon_i, \epsilon_j)$ denotes the number of edges along the path separating nodes ϵ_i and ϵ_j. The category locality is negative or equal to zero. Values that are closer to 0 indicate that the instances of category

c are concentrated in a few adjacent nodes, and negative values indicate that the category instances are more dispersed in the tree. We define the locality as the weighted average of the category locality, where the weights are the category instance frequencies.

We note that each of these objectives can generally be improved on the account of the other: locality can usually be improved by joining nodes (which in general makes purity worse), and purity can usually be improved by splitting nodes (which in general makes locality worse). Therefore, we argue that a desirable hierarchy should offer an acceptable compromise between these two performance measures.

5 Experimental results

In this section we learn the attribute hierarchy using our proposed ATP algorithm. In order to evaluate the performance we evaluate the ATP as a hierarchical clustering algorithm, and compare it to the FBLM and AHC. We use subsets of the PASCAL VOC2008, and SUN09 datasets, for which attribute annotations are available. We learn hierarchies using the ground truth attribute annotation of the training set, and using the attribute scores obtained for the image instances in the testing set, where the attribute detectors are trained using the training set. We used the FBLM implementation which is available online. Our implementation of the ATP is based the TSSBP implementation which is available online, where we extended it to implement our ATP generative model. We used the AHC implementation available at (Mullner,), where we used the average distance metric, which is also known as the *Unweighted Pair Group Method with Arithmetic Mean* (UMPGA) (Murtagh, 1984).

5.1 Object category hierarchy

Here we consider the PASCAL VOC 2008 dataset. We use the bounding boxes and attribute annotation data that were collected in (Farhadi et al., 2009), and are available online, along with the low-level image features. Each of the training and testing sets contains over 6000 instances of the object classes: person, bird, cat, cow, dog, horse, sheep, airplane, bicycle, boat, bus, car, motorcycle, train, bottle, chair, dining-table, potted-plant, sofa, and tv/monitor. We used the annotation and features available for the training set, to train the attribute detectors using a linear SVM classifier (Fan et al., 2008). We used 88 attributes, which included 24 attributes in addition to those used in (Farhadi et al., 2009): "pet", "vehicle", "alive", "animal", and the remaining 20 attributes were identical to the object classes. The annotation for the first 4 additional attributes was inferred from the object classes. In all the experiments presented here, we ran the Markov chain for 10,000 iterations and used the tree and model parameters from the final iteration.

The attribute hierarchies for the PASCAL dataset are shown in Figure 3, when using the annotation for the training set, and when using the attribute scores obtained for the testing set. The hierarchies were obtained by thresholding $h_\epsilon^{(d)}$ with the threshold parameter 0.7 (this parameter is only used to create the visualization, and it is not used when learning the hierarchies), and only displaying the attributes that are not already associated with an ancestor node. It can be seen that the attribute hierarchies can accurately capture the semantic space that is represented by the 20 categories in the PASCAL dataset. An important observation is that attributes which are associated with more categories, such as alive or vehicle, are assigned to nodes that are closer to the root node, as compared to more specialized attributes such as eye or window.

In order to evaluate the performance of the attribute hierarchies quantitatively, we use the ground truth category hierarchy for the 20 categories in the PASCAL dataset, which is available at (Binder et al., 2012), and is shown in Figure 4. In Figure 5 we show the AEE performance measure, which we discussed in the previous section, for the different hierarchical clustering algorithms which we consider here. It can be seen that for the AHC, the AEE is very sensitive to the threshold parameter, which effectively determines the number of clusters. A poor choice of the parameter can adversely affect the performance significantly. On the other hand, the performance of the ATP and FBLM is significantly less sensitive to the choice of the hyper-parameters, since all the parameters are learned in a Bayesian fashion with weak dependence on the hyper-parameters. This is demonstrated for the ATP in Section 5.1.1. The ATP significantly improves the AEE as com-

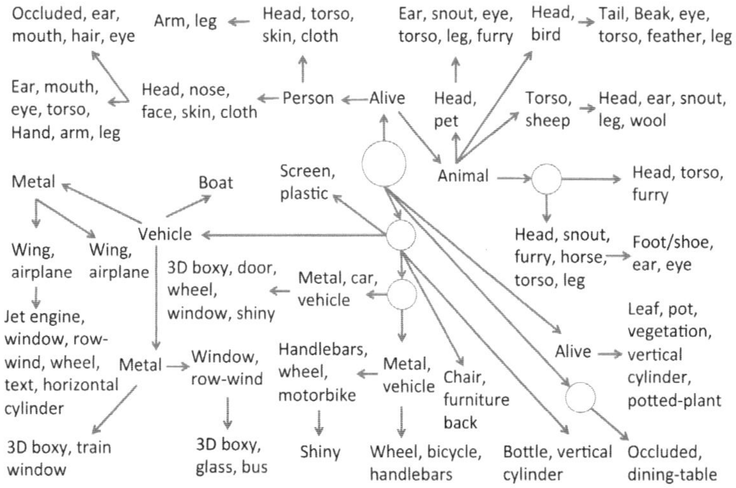

(a) Using the attribute annotation of the training set.

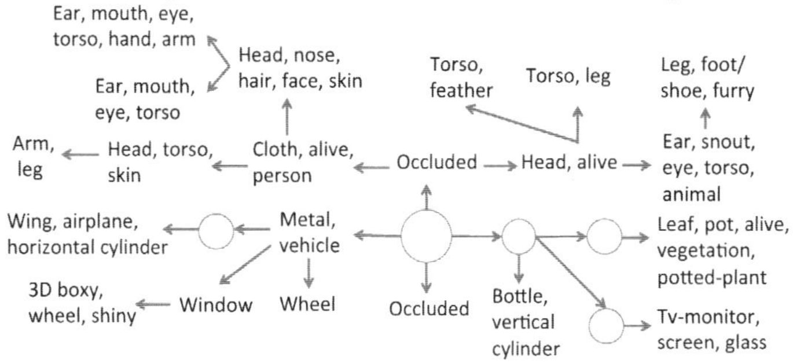

(b) Using the attribute scores of the testing set.

Figure 3: Attribute hierarchy learned for the PASCAL dataset, using the (a) attribute annotation available for the training set, and (b) attribute scores obtained by applying the attribute detectors to the image instances of the testing set. The largest circle denotes the root node.

pared to the FBLM, both for the training and testing sets. We also note, that for the ATP, the AEE obtained for the training set is better than that obtained using the testing set's attribute scores (training: 1.76, testing: 2.82), which is consistent with our expectation. This is not the case for the FBLM (training: 6.55, testing: 5.63).

5.1.1 Sensitivity to hyper-parameters

In order to validate our claim that the ATP is highly insensitive to the choice of hyper-parameters, we performed experiments with different hyper-parameter values. In Table 1 we compare the performance when using different values for the hyper-parameters a, and b in (4). It can be seen that when comparing to AHC in Figure 5, the ATP is significantly less sensitive to the choice of hyper-parameters. When comparing to the FBLM, even for the the worst choice of a, b the AEE is still significantly better.

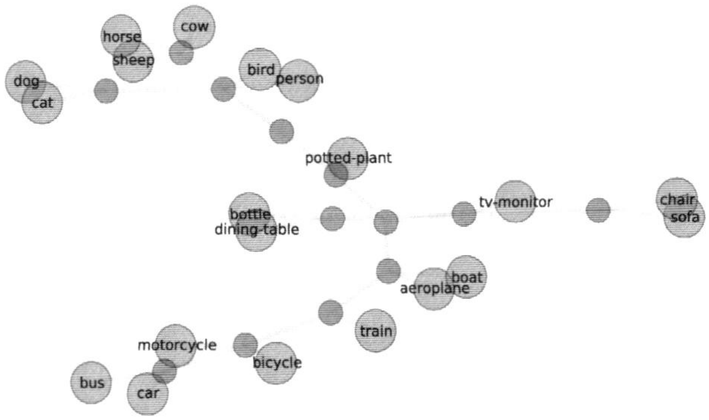

Figure 4: The ground truth category hierarchy, for the 20 categories in the PASCAL dataset.

5.2 Scene category hierarchy

Here we used the SUN09 dataset which is comprised of indoor and outdoor scenes. We use the training

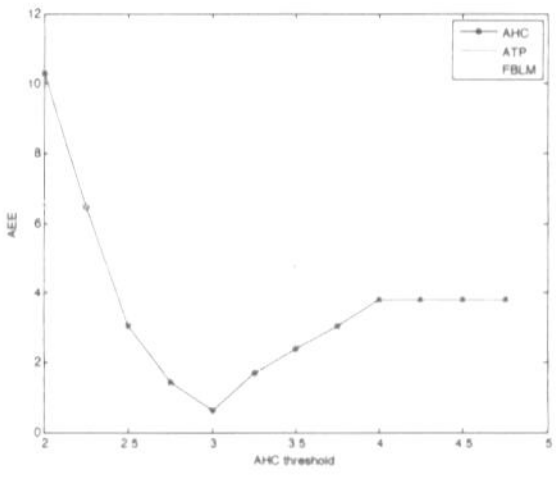

(a) Training

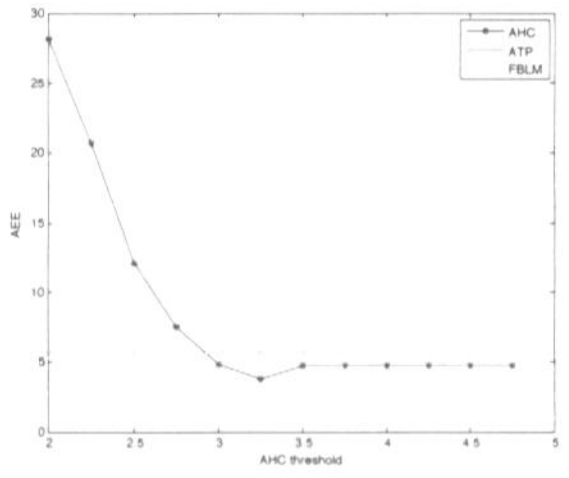

(b) Testing

Figure 5: The average edge error (AEE) (10) vs. the AHC threshold parameter, for the hierarchies learned using the (a) training set's attribute annotations, and (b) attribute detectors applied to the testing set image instances. Smaller values indicate better performance. It can be seen that our ATP algorithm outperforms the FBLM, and unlike the AHC, it is not as sensitive to the choice of the hyper-parameters.

Table 1: Average edge error using the attribute annotation of the training set, for different hyper-parameters.

a	b	AEE
1	10	1.97
5	5	1.93
10	5	1.76
10	10	1.585
10	20	1.569

and testing sets which were used in (Myung et al., 2012), each containing over 4000 images. The annotation of 111 objects in the training set, and object detector scores for the testing set, are available online. Objects in the scene have the role of attributes in describing the scene. The object classifiers were trained using logistic regression classifiers based on Gist features that were extracted from the training set.

Since the ground truth category hierarchy is unavailable for this dataset, we use the locality and purity criteria, which we described in the previous section. We computed both of these measures with respect to the indoor and outdoor categories. Figure 6 shows the locality and purity measures for the training and testing sets. It can be seen that the AHC is very sensitive to the threshold parameter, and can produce unsatisfactory performance for a wide range of parameter values. The FBLM slightly outperforms the ATP with respect to the purity measure, however, its locality is very poor. Therefore, we conclude that the ATP provides an improved compromise with respect to the two criteria, which shows that the ATP captures the properties of a desirable hierarchy better than the FBLM.

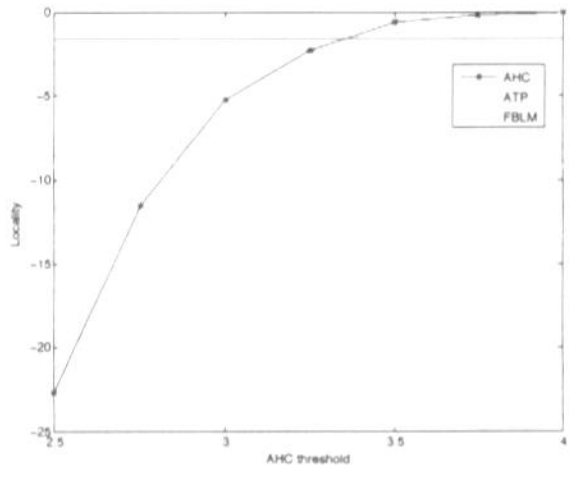

(a) Training- Locality

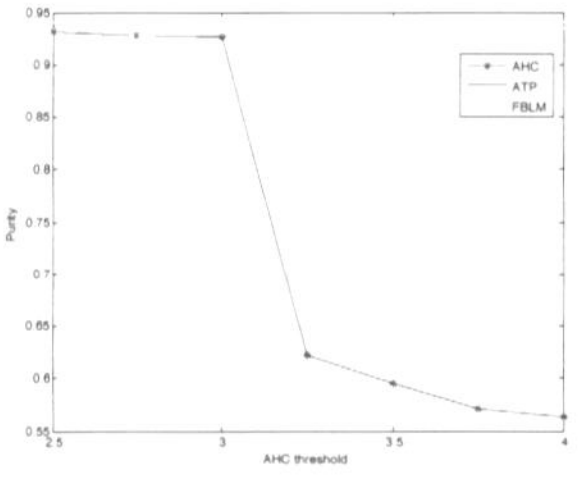

(b) Training- Purity

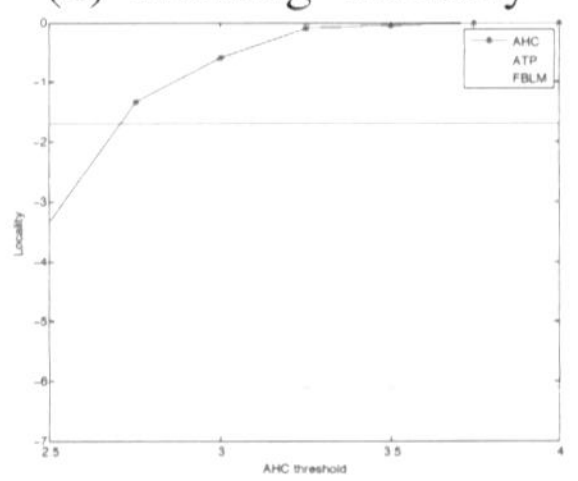

(c) Testing- Locality

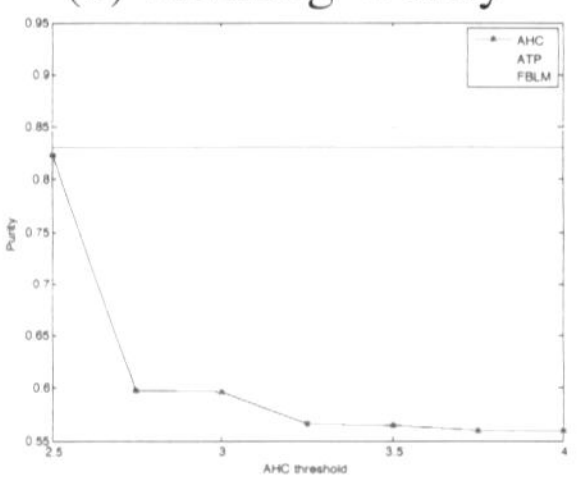

(d) Testing- Purity

Figure 6: The locality and purity measures vs. the AHC threshold parameter, using the training set's attribute annotation, and for the testing set's attribute scores. Larger values indicate better performance. It can be seen that our ATP has significantly better locality, and only slightly worse purity, compared to the FBLM. Furthermore, the performance of the AHC depends significantly on the choice of threshold parameter.

6 Conclusions

We developed an algorithm, which we refer to as the attribute tree process (ATP), that uses an attribute based representation to learn a hierarchy of linguistic descriptions, and can be used to describe a visual dataset verbally. In order to quantitatively evaluate the performance of our algorithm, we proposed appropriate performance metrics for the cases where the ground truth category hierarchy is known, and when it is unknown. We compared the ATP's performance as a hierarchical clustering algorithm to other competing methods, and demonstrated that our method can more accurately capture the ground truth semantic distance between the different categories. Furthermore, we demonstrated that our method has weak sensitivity to the choice of hyper-parameters.

Acknowledgments

We acknowledge the support of the NSF Grant CPS-0931474.

References

[Adams et al.2010] R. P. Adams, Z. Ghahramani, and M. I. Jordan. 2010. Tree-Structured Stick Breaking for Hierarchical Data. *NIPS*.

[Bart et al.2011] E. Bart, and M. Welling, and P. Perona. 2011. Unsupervised organization of Image Collections: Taxonomies and Beyond. *IEEE Tran. on PAMI,* 33(11):2302–2315.

[Berg et al.2011] T. L. Berg, A. C. Berg and J. Shih. 2010. Automatic Attribute Discovery and Characterization from Noisy Web Data. *CVPR*.

[Binder et al.2012] A. Binder, K. R. Muller, and M. Kawanabe. 2012. On Taxonomies for Multi-class Image Categorization. *International Journal of Computer Vision,* 99:281–301.

[Fan et al.2008] R. Fan, K. Chang, C. Hsieh, X. Wang, and C. Lin. 2008. LIBLINEAR: A Library for Large Linear Classification. *Journal of Machine Learning Research,* 9:1871–1874.

[Farhadi et al.2009] A. Farhadi, I. Endres, D. Hoiem, and David Forsyth. 2009. Describing objects by their attributes. *CVPR*.

[Ferrari & Zisserman2007] V. Ferrari and A. Zisserman. 2010. Learning Visual Attributes. *CVPR*.

[Jain & Dubes1988 p. 59] A. K. Jain and R. C. Dubes. 1988. *Algorithms for Clustering Data.* Prentice-Hall, Englewood Cliffs, NJ.

[Lampert et al.2009] C. H. Lampert, H. Nickisch, and S. Harmeling. 2009. Learning to detect unseen object classes by between class attribute transfer. *CVPR*.

[Li et al.2010] L. J. Li, and C. Wang, and Y. Lim, and D. M. Blei, and L. Fei-Fei. 2010. Building and using a semantivisual image hierarchy. *CVPR*.

[Manning et al.2009 p. 357] C. D. Manning, P. Raghavan, and H. Schtze. 2009. *An Introduction to information retrieval.* Available online at http://nlp.stanford.edu/IR-book/.

[Mullner] D. Mulner. fastcluster: Fast hierarchical clustering routines for R and Python. *http://math.stanford.edu/ muellner/index.html.*

[Murtagh1984] F. Murtagh. 1984. Complexities of Hierarchic Clustering Algorithms: the state of the art. *Computational Statistics Quarterly,* 1: 101–113.

[Myung et al.2012] M. J. Choi, A. Torralba and A. S. Willsky. 2012. A Tree-Based Context Model for Object Recognition. *IEEE Tran. on PAMI,* 34(2):240–252.

[Neal2000] R. Neal. 2000. Nonparametric factor analysis with beta process priors. *Annals of Statistics,* 31:705–767.

[Paisley & Carin2009] J. W. Paisley, and L. Carin. 2009. Nonparametric factor analysis with beta process priors. *ICML*.

[Parikh & Grauman2011] P. Devi and G. Kristen. 2011. Interactively building a discriminative vocabulary of nameable attributes. *CVPR*.

[Sivic et al.2008] J. Sivic, and B. C. Russel, and A. Zisserman, and W. T. Freeman, and A. A. Efros. 2008. Unsupervised Discovery of visual object class hierarchies. *CVPR*.

[Teh et al.2006] Y. W. Teh and M. I. Jordan and M. J. Beal and D. M. Blei. 2006. Hierarchical Dirichlet Processes. *Journal of the American Statistical Association,* 101(476):1566–1581.

[Thibaux & Jordan2007] R. Thibaux and M. I. Jordan. 2007. Hierarchical Beta Processes and the Indian Buffet Process. *AISTATS*.

Author Index